10855619

The Lazy Hostess

About the Author

Babe Scott is a self-described 'kitchen vixen' on a mission to put the flirt back into finger food. She's living proof that anyone can become an entertaining queen, even if they weren't born with the cooking gene. This stovetop siren transformed herself from a kitchen biohazard into a culinary whizz who can whip up dishes for every occasion with ease – while still having fun along the way.

This martini-loving minx is also an inventive mixologist and has created luscious libations for the likes of *Glamour*, Bridefinds.com, and *Glo*. She posts a weekly cocktail on her Facebook page for her 16,000-plus followers, as well as dishing up decadent recipes and side servings of humor. Babe also blogs for HuffingtonPost.com and has written for CNNLiving.com, YourTango.com and other online sites, while her lifestyle advice has appeared on More.com, Yahoo! Shine, Match.com, MSN Lifestyle and in other popular media.

Apart from her party-throwing prowess, Babe is also a card-carrying manthropologist. She previously authored a book called *Delicious Dating* and has aired her saucy views on dating and mating on a range of shows from Pix11 *Morning News* to 7 *Live* San Francisco. She also edited the *Dating Survival Guide*, a complete man manual for Aussie seductresses and dispensed advice for the lovelorn on top-rated down-under shows.

Prior to packing up her cocktail shaker and heading Stateside, Babe published magazines in her native Australia, launching over 30 titles on everything from fashion to food to nightlife.

Babe lives in New York with her daughter, Bondi, and her two precocious pooches, Sweetie and Dahling.

For more information about Babe, visit her website at www.babescott.com, her Facebook page at www.facebook.com/lazyhostess, or @thelazyhostess on Twitter.

The Lazy Hostess

Babe Scott

BANTAM PRESS

LONDON · TORONTO · SYDNEY · AUCKLAND · JOHANNESBURG

TRANSWORLD PUBLISHERS
61–63 Uxbridge Road, London W5 5SA
A Random House Group Company
www.transworldbooks.co.uk

First published in Great Britain
in 2013 by Bantam Press
an imprint of Transworld Publishers

Copyright © 2013 Babe Scott

Babe Scott has asserted her right under the Copyright,
Designs and Patents Act 1988 to be identified as the author of this work.

A CIP catalogue record for this book
is available from the British Library.

ISBN 9780593072646

This book is sold subject to the condition that it shall not,
by way of trade or otherwise, be lent, resold, hired out,
or otherwise circulated without the publisher's prior
consent in any form of binding or cover other than that
in which it is published and without a similar condition,
including this condition, being imposed on the
subsequent purchaser.

Addresses for Random House Group Ltd companies outside the UK
can be found at: www.randomhouse.co.uk
The Random House Group Ltd Reg. No. 954009

Illustrations by Chuck Gonzales
Photographs by Dorothy Shi
Typeset by Envydesign

Printed and bound in
China by Toppan Leefung Printing Limited, China

2 4 6 8 10 9 7 5 3 1

This book is dedicated to the memory of my mother, Pat, who taught me the true meaning of hospitality.

'I like to have a martini,
two at the very most.
After three I'm under
the table, after four I'm
under my host.'
– Dorothy Parker

Contents

'Grab your saucepans, girls.

It's time to put the FLIRT

into finger food.'

Hello, Sister

It's Your New Best Friend Here

A tiny detail like being clueless about cooking shouldn't stop you from becoming a cocktail party queen. No matter how domestically challenged you are, The Lazy Hostess will show you how to get your Hostess on.

Who am I? And what on earth is this book? Quite simply, I'm the laziest ho in the entire universe, especially when it comes to entertaining. And yet, I have a knack for throwing soirées and dinner parties that are wildly successful, at least when measured in laughter, litres of wine and memories I can hold my friends to ransom with. I'm not a chef, nor do I have any culinary credentials, but I do know how to feed the hungry hordes while barely lifting a finger or breaking the budget. And, more importantly, I've worked out how to have one hell of a good time. (Number-one rule: a happy hostess makes for a happy occasion!)

I've always loved to entertain. Even back when I couldn't cook without risk to life and limb, I was a cocktail-party queen. I would warn guests that they should don non-flammable clothing, but they still came in droves and talked about my soirées for years afterwards in terms that would make Martha Stewart greener than the Grinch. Since those days, I've learned to make food that doesn't look like it's been charred in Chernobyl and have developed enough skill in the kitchen that I can manage to put something together to satisfy most palates and occasions.

Although I'm no longer on a first-name basis with the local fire brigade (a shame, because they are total stud muffins) and my friends no longer brush up on their first aid before coming over for cocktails and canapés, I'm still a slatternly bitch when it comes to the stove top. For me, it's about cooking to love, not loving to cook. I don't want to spend a cent more or a second longer in the kitchen than I have to. And I don't want to make anything so complicated that I can't throw it together while watching a soap and swigging my favourite Chardonnay with a girlfriend.

'*Food is just an* **ACCESSORY.**' ♥

Hello, Sister xi

♥ ♥ ♥

This book is for domestically challenged divas who have always dreamed of entertaining but who have an allergy to cooking so severe it practically requires doses of Ephedrine. It's a lifesaving tome for those of us who weren't born with the cooking gene and for whom the thought of having friends over for drinks inspires panic attacks. Help is finally at hand for you, my cocktail-swilling sisters.

The Lazy Hostess takes the fear out of food and puts the 'fun' back in, letting you woo the world with your HOspitality. It puts the curve back into cooking and the frou-frou into frugal. It aims to be not just a book, but a new best friend. It recognizes that food is just an accessory. Let's face it – entertaining is mostly an excuse to put on our Sunday best and play the siren rather than sweating it out over the stove top.

I hope you'll consider this book a saucy girlfriend in ink, one that will be with you every mincing step of the way to ensure you have an intoxicating evening. In it, you'll find laid out on a platter everything you need to know to become the hostess with the mostest with a minimum of effort, so you can conserve your energy for consuming cocktails. To ensure you look and feel your queenly best, it's got infallible fashion ideas as well as tips to get you in the party mood. I'll

*'Consider this book a **GIRLFRIEND** in ink.'* ♥

also help you create a festive atmosphere with suggestions for signature cocktails, sprucing up your abode and soundtracks for every occasion.

It doesn't stop there. On my website – babescott.com – you can download irresistible invitations, as well as tantalizing placemats and coasters. No crêpe is left unturned in showing you how to become the queen of your social scene.

The only thing this book doesn't do is wash up afterwards. (Hopefully, you have an OCD friend who can help you attend to that.) *The Lazy Hostess* will show you how to have a royal good time.

DOWNLOAD
IRRESISTIBLE
INVITATIONS ON
MY WEBSITE
BABESCOTT.COM.

How to conquer the world

without leaving home

or risking a hangnail.

Putting the

HO

into

Hostess

1

The Art of Being a Happy Hostess

The real purpose of entertaining is to amuse the hostess. It's not about being a domestic drone but being a diva. The Lazy Hostess explains the art of being a cocktail-party queen.

Entertaining should be all about the hostess. We entertain to amuse ourselves not prove ourselves. The hostess reigns supreme. She is the queen of the occasion, and queens don't risk a hangnail or a stress-induced headache from slaving over a hot stove. They make things easy on themselves and exude elegance and grace (at least until they fall over after too many chocolate martinis).

And queens certainly don't spend all their time in the kitchen. They need to be on hand to hold court with their friends and loyal subjects and to lead the festivities. Being a cocktail-party queen is not about being a cordon bleu cook or a domestic drone.

It has nothing to do with making complicated canapés or searching high and low to find fussy ingredients. We don't want to exert ourselves beyond the local supermarket. If your friends want to eat edible flowers they can help themselves from the vase.

Cheers big ears!

Nor is it about trying to impress your guests or flashing crystal glassware. It doesn't matter if you drink from plastic cups, as long as you do it with aplomb. Being a party queen is not about any notion of perfection. Nor should throwing spectacular soirées overstretch your wallet. The secret to being a great hostess isn't about being fancy but rather about making one and all feel welcome. It's about opening your heart and pantry to the world and inviting it in.

The key to a great night is making enjoyment your priority, particularly your own. A cocktail party is a chance to inject a little glamour into our lives and lounges. It's an opportunity to throw off the shackles of the mundane and become minxes. The best reasons to throw a shindig are to show off our favourite threads and to watch our friends slowly make fools of themselves.

It's about fun and fashion and food, in that order, with food in a laggardly third place. Being a great hostess is less about what you put on a plate than how you present yourself and preside over the festivities. We are not mad *hausfraus* but party hos and we should plan the night accordingly.

Get Frocked

It all starts with the outfit. The fashion ensemble is the star of the night, or at least your co-star. The evening should ideally be sparked by some sort of fashion inspiration. I have a girlfriend who has orchestrated entire nights around a pair of earrings. Find something you are excited to wear and create an occasion around it.

For me, it's all about the frock. In case you don't know

'A frock is a dress with a little bit of **DIVA** *in it.'* ❤

the difference between a frock and a dress, both of which may very well emerge from the same rack in a department store, the easiest way to explain it is this: a dress is what you wear to work or when you're returning library books, whereas a frock has mystical powers. It's a dress with a little bit of diva in it. It's something that, when you put it on, your whole personality lights up like a Broadway stage.

Marilyn Monroe wore frocks. So did Ava Gardner. And that little black slip that Audrey Hepburn made iconic in *Breakfast at Tiffany's* was definitely a frock. Think of your dinner party as a mini movie with you as the main character. No film ever made history with a heroine wearing a pair of old dungarees and flat shoes. Likewise, I don't care if you give away free foie gras and French champagne; if you can't be bothered to dress with a little bit of flair, then the evening will fall as flat as the soles of your sensible shoes. My advice to you is to 'Get FROCKED'.

If you find facing down your wardrobe a little frightening, or if your closet needs some serious style CPR, then don't worry – I will help you find your entertaining alter-ego. That's what being new best friends is all about. There's no favour too small.

You'll find plenty of fashion advice in these luminous pages to help you assemble the perfect outfit for every occasion, whatever your budget. Divas come in all shapes and sizes: skinny, curvy and inbetweeny. It's all about flaunting your assets and feeling good. No self-respecting hostess wants to be upstaged by her menu.

Put Fun on the Menu

Entertaining is about having fun and making friends while under the influence. It's far more intimate to have people over than to go out to a venue. It connects you and your new acquaintances, friends and cohorts in a deeper way. It also means that you can hold court in your lounge. These people, who have given themselves up to your hospitality, are your veritable social hostages for the night. Their fate is in your hands. The hostess sets the tone for the evening, from the dress code, to the drinks, to the food, to the party favours.

The hostess is the social conductor, like Spielberg orchestrating his actors. The hostess rules the roost. In a tiny way, you get to know how God feels. I like to think of entertaining as an ongoing social experiment where you get a

Light up your life.

bunch of miscellaneous misfits together, add food and alcohol, then stand back and wait for the blast. Sometimes it's just a few fireworks, but sometimes there's true social combustion.

The funny things that happen at a cocktail party could never be replicated in a bar. You can make friends for life in one night. Love affairs can ignite. A shy person can burst into spontaneous song. An uptight lawyer can start doing the limbo on the dance floor. It's these moments that we live for … and you shouldn't let a small detail like being domestically insane stop you from having them.

It's a myth that you have to master haute cuisine, own blemish-free crockery, or memorize *Debrett's Guide to Etiquette* to be a great hostess. In fact, the opposite is true. The last thing you want is for people to be on their best behaviour. The great moments at a cocktail party happen when your guests loosen up and you get to glimpse their alter-egos. That is, you get to see them *misbehave* and get up to all sorts of naughtiness.

*'If you know how to put together a **SIGNATURE COCKTAIL**, then you're well on your way!'* ♥

The key to being a great hostess is simply to be committed to having fun with friends. It's all about the spirit in which you present the evening. Fun and frivolity should be your maxim. Leave the office behind and let the moon rule. If you manage this, then your efforts can't fail to entertain.

Easy Recipes for Kitchen Minxes

Now that we have donned the right mindset towards our menus, there are plenty of simple, scrumptious recipe options that won't cause an ounce of perspiration or even exasperation. This survival bible for slothful yet sizzling hostesses features recipes so simple that even a primary-school kid could make them.

There are also cheat sheets for when you can't be bothered to cook at all and just want to order ready-made food from your local grocer or supermarket. I've included tips and serving suggestions so you can posh up your shop-bought items to make them look like you have made them yourself.

The key to stress-free entertaining is to make cooking easy so you can focus on fun. The second secret is preparation. If everything is on hand, then you don't have to go scrambling. You don't want to be stuck in the kitchen when your guests are arriving, or passed out on the couch with the smelling salts from nervous exhaustion.

This book has it all planned out for you so that the prep can be done well ahead and there will still be time for a long bubble bath as well as all the other primping and preening necessary to make you look and feel like a queen before your guests arrive at the door. I have come up with more menu options than you will ever need to know. Frankly, you don't have to master more than a handful of recipes to become a renowned hostess. If you can put out a few hors d'oeuvres and a signature cocktail, then you are well on your way. After a few aperitifs, your guests will barely register what they're eating anyway. Rest assured, the recipes in this book are delicious; but just remember you aren't competing for a *Masterchef* title. You are simply showing your friends a good time.

So go forth and have fun while entertaining. Invite your friends, potential new squeezes, neighbours, the bank manager, your inbred cousin and assorted rent-a-crowd over for a bite. They will be begging you to let them come back for seconds.

2

The 7 Habits of Highly Stress-free Hostesses

Recruit a friend to play the role of sous chef.

here is nothing lonelier than cooking solo, especially when you don't know your left elbow from an artichoke. I never cook alone. It's as much fun as a private joke. Recruit a friend with culinary talents to be your sous chef. Cooking with a friend turns the preparation itself into a social event. It means you will have someone to chop onions and share tall stories with as well as confer on the menu. He or she can also make sure you stay on course and don't get distracted and incinerate the meal. They can also teach you all their tips and tricks, like making sure the oven is turned on.

Make sure you both taste everything so you can compare notes on flavours. Having someone else to consult will give you the confidence to add a little twist here and there to suit your own tastes. Spending time in the kitchen is also a great bonding exercise and you two, or even three, can share a spot of sherry to get in the mood before the guests arrive.

'Cooking with a friend turns the preparation itself into a **SOCIAL EVENT**.*'* ❤

I guarantee you will learn more about your foodie friends in the time it takes to put together your finger food menu than if you had known them for years. There's something about the camaraderie of the kitchen that inspires confidences. But, remember, what goes on over the stovetop stays over the stovetop. It's like a confessional with cocktails.

You and your Chardonnay support group can also make up delicious-sounding names for your dishes. Think about the mood you want to create so you can give your hors d'oeuvres the right monikers. For example, a shy, stuffed celery stick can be transformed into its after-dark alter-ego simply with a devilish dusting of paprika and a new nocturnal nom de plume such as 'Fifty Shades of Celery'.

Pre-plan the evening.

 recommend buying all the ingredients a day or more before the soirée. There is nothing more stressful than shopping on the day of a party. It's more important that you have time to relax, do your nails and douse yourself with perfume. You want to look and feel perfectly edible. You don't want to be outshone by the hors d'oeuvres.

I suggest preparing everything you can ahead of time. Any items you can pre-cook and freeze, do so on a rainy day with a friend. Then you can simply defrost and reheat them on the evening. It's also better to spruce up your space and put together your party playlist at least the day before. And make sure at least a few items can be served at room temperature.

Make sure you have pre-thought everything else so you don't have any last-minute panic attacks. The soundtracks and any sprucing up are also best done at least the day before. Make sure your kitchen cohort arrives early to help with the pre-heating and plating, and that you have a bunch of platters to put things on. This way, you will get to spend most of the day preening.

'*It's more important that you have time to* **RELAX, DO YOUR NAILS AND DOUSE YOURSELF WITH PERFUME.**'♥

If you do forget anything on the appointed evening, just pour yourself another drink and don't worry. Throw up your hands and let someone else take care of it.

Delegate like a true diva.

Friends love showing off their talents, so make sure you avail yourself of any skills they might have. I have friends who have made a lifestyle out of living off other people's largesse, and it seems only fair to me that they sing for their supper in return. For instance, I have a male friend, let's call him 'Scott

Free', who almost never forks out for food or even springs for a bottle of plonk. Even so, he is amusing and he can sing. Scott Free once won an Elvis competition in Vegas and has an incredible set of vocal cords, so I always make sure my frugal friend wears his Elvis jacket and brings along his guitar to help entertain the guests.

Make sure you delegate someone the role of official photographer. There is always some friend who thinks of themselves as an aspiring Mario Testino or David Bailey who will enjoy taking paparazzi-style snaps. Being the group happy-snapper is a great ticket to popularity as everyone (or at least all my friends) loves posing. This way you should have some great photos to mount on your wall of infamy and also to put in your party scrapbook later.

'You might have a friend who is great at DECORATING so get her to help you create a festive atmosphere.' ❤

Palm off whatever other tawdry tasks you can too. For instance, you might have a friend who is great at decorating, so get her to help you create a festive atmosphere. Some other acquaintance may have a fantastic CD collection . . . you follow my drift. Delegate like a cocktail-party diva. This way everybody gets to feel like part of the event and his or her respective talents get recognized. Just make sure you point out and applaud each contributor's efforts at some point during the evening. This also gives them plenty of talking points and gives you a good excuse to raise multiple toasts.

Serve an icebreaker signature cocktail.

*N*othing kickstarts a party better than serving your guests a signature cocktail at the door. It's like giving them a dose of rocket propellant. It loosens people up straight off the bat and creates a great icebreaker by giving them something to talk about. It also adds a touch of pizzazz.

Make up a fabulous name for your libation that helps set the right tone for the evening. A good trick is to give it a slight twist and name it after yourself – for instance, the 'Janetini'. This will lend it a little of your sparkling personality. Or call it something seductive like the 'Sexytini' and tell everyone this magical mix is an 'aphrodisiac in a glass'. Nothing like the power of suggestion. And everyone can blame your mystical potion later for their misbehaviour.

A signature cocktail is also a great way to introduce your friends to your own recipe for liquid bliss. And if you don't know what the recipe for nirvana is yet, well there are plenty of inexpensive, easy recipes in this book that you can adopt as your signature sip.

It's easy to concoct a great ice-breaking elixir. You don't have to

'Make up a **FABULOUS** *name for your elixir that helps set the right tone for the evening.'* ❤

spend the earth to create a posh-seeming cocktail. Most great cocktails contain only two or three simple ingredients. In fact, many famous drinks were invented by ingenious hosts who created their own concoctions (usually after running out of other ingredients). If your guests are already a little lubricated, they will be far more receptive to your culinary offerings.

Another way to set the right tone straight off is to have a dress code. It's all about flaunting our frocks and putting on the ritz. I like to pretend I am Princess Margaret holding court on the island of Mustique, or I will take fashion inspiration from Ginger Rogers or my all-time favourite fashion icon ('I'm not bad, I'm just drawn that way') Jessica Rabbit. Thank God for push-up bras and shapewear. Dressing up is half the fun. Otherwise, you may as well go out and eat a falafel at your local food stand. And where's the romance in that?

Don't let your guests slack off in the sartorial stakes either. Let them know in plenty of time so they can plan their get-ups. And let the guys know that they can't be slobs. Men need a lot of direction generally. The poor dears are very binary-coded, so be really specific. If you are going through a Cary Grant phase, then give them a little

'Thank God for **PUSH-UP BRAS** *and* **SHAPEWEAR.** *Dressing up is half the fun.'* ♥

direction on what to wear and even suggestions on how to style their hair. At the very least, they should dress to impress. Advise them to don an outfit they would wear to a restaurant rather than a pub: a button-up shirt, dress trousers and decent shoes. Don't discourage them from wearing black tie or any other form of finery. The exception would only be if the guy is completely 'abtastic', in which case he may be allowed to go shirtless (but caliper test him first to ensure it's an appetizing sight).

Let the games begin.

Running a cocktail party is akin to running a daycare for delinquent children. I generally find guests regress to an infantile state as the night wears on. Just like controlling a hyperactive class of under-fives, you must make sure your charges are adequately fed and watered or they will become fractious.

It's equally important that they get a chance to burn off steam. Dancing is key. Change the soundtrack to one with a little faster tempo as the night wears on and you have all imbibed a few cocktails. Clear a few chairs and create an improvised dance floor. Check out our 'Dance Your Ass Off' party mix at www.babescott.com section for some compulsive dance tracks.

I find having some fun activities on hand also helps. For instance, buy a karaoke machine from Toys R Us and let your friends take turns warbling. You may want a giant hook to get some of the keener songsters to leave the microphone, but it's guaranteed hilarity.

'There are plenty of games from limbo to charades you can play to engage your guests.' ❤

There are plenty of other games, from limbo to charades, which you can play to engage your guests. One idea is to give everyone someone else's keys so they have to talk to other guests to find them. Start rumours, pass on made-up compliments from other guests, do anything you can to get your guests mingling.

Start a cocktail-party guest book.

Finally, start a guest book that your friends can write in before they leave. Try to select the ideal time for them to make the most flattering comments. This should be when they are drunk enough to be generous with their superlatives but not so loose they can barely string a sentence together. I would suggest the ideal time is after a few beverages but before they start bopping on the dance floor. Encourage them to put into words what a fabulous time they had and let them know that they can't be effusive enough, that high-flying fits of hyperbole are more than welcome. It's a good idea to offer an amazing review of a four-star restaurant as an example to help them find their flow.

Leave a column for 'compliments to the hostess' so they can also tell you how simply adorable you are. Leave a thesaurus next to the guest book in case they are *'Wonderful is a word that can never be worn out.'* ❤ struggling to find the right adjectives. I like to leave mine open at a page that may prompt their imagination. Perhaps highlight the word 'wonderful' – it's a word that can never be worn out.

Leave room after these tributes to a terrific evening for photos and other mementoes of the night. It's a way of collecting all the unforgettable memories and majestic moments of your party in one star-kissed scrapbook.

This written record will serve as a lovely memento of the evening. It makes for entertaining reading, as well as providing a testimony to your fabulousness and your status as a hostess with the mostest.

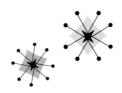

The kitchen is the beating heart of your home.

*If it's growing cobwebs, chances are
your social life is too. I'll show you how to
clear the cobwebs and get cooking.*

3

Conquer Your Kitchen

*A*lbert Einstein once famously quipped, 'Imagination is more important than knowledge.' It's also more important than kitchen equipment. Entertaining is all about the art of improvisation. Necessity is the mother of invention and also of inventive soirées. You don't need cutting-edge appliances, a full set of Ninja-sharp knives or crystal wine glasses. Nor do you need to take out an equity loan in preparation for a visit to Fortnum & Mason.

It's possible to cook with very few tools and limited easy-to-find ingredients while still providing delicious food. Similarly, it doesn't matter if your guests drink out of mismatched glassware or even paper cups. In fact, I think some mismatching elements add to the ambience. It also makes it easier for friends to find their glasses if none look alike.

I personally enjoy collecting a jumbled assortment of vintage glassware sourced from charity shops. Nothing matches at my parties, from the plates to the people I invite. I enjoy mixing different personalities just as I do everything else. It makes for a more interesting evening by adding a social wild-card element.

I'm also not averse to using plastic cups, in addition to glassware for a bigger event. You can even get plastic martini or champagne glasses. This means you won't have to worry when a few plates or cocktail glasses go flying. Instead, you can celebrate the fact, as broken glassware is a good barometer of a sizzling party.

You too can host all manner of soirées even if your kitchen is as underequipped as a college freshman at a cougar convention. It doesn't even matter if you possess barely any furniture. For instance, two furniture-challenged girlfriends of mine had a housewarming picnic on the floor of their new apartment. It was all very 'Arabian Nights', with pillows thrown everywhere, candles and incense. They borrowed such a varied range of glassware and crockery that the floor setting looked like a Turkish garage sale. It all added to the wonderful atmosphere. One of them even gave an impromptu belly dance.

Talking of other resourceful cooks, I have an Aussie friend called Phil who makes amazing dinners with a single pot and an ancient frying pan. This wandering artist travels all over the outback, pitching tents in remote places, miles from any grocery store. He calls himself the 'Camp Cook' because he can pull a few cans and other goodies out of an ice box, build a fire out of fallen tree branches and minutes later have put together a yummy casserole (not to mention, he's also as camp as a row of tents). Phil could host a gourmet cocktail party on the set of *Survivor*.

That isn't to say you shouldn't put together a wish list of what you want for your dream kitchen or cocktail bar. Some lovely stemware can lift the spirits and certain appliances can make your job in the kitchen much easier, leaving you more time to mingle with your guests. Later in this chapter, I've given a rundown of the kitchen items that will cover you for nearly every occasion. Don't let this list scare you. You can build your kitchen arsenal over time and a lot of these things can be bought in sets.

If you are completely bereft of utensils, there is always the option to make the Camp Cook's One-Pot Dinner Party or the Pizza Dinner Party described later in this chapter. You can also beg, borrow or steal the equipment you need just for each occasion rather than getting everything in one fell swoop. It's amazing what people will donate if you bribe them with the promise of a couple of medicinal beverages and some delicious hors d'oeuvres.

Make Over Your Kitchen

Think of your kitchen as an extension of you. It should be full of inviting odours, not scary ones. There is nothing worse than walking into someone's kitchen and wishing you'd been to the doctor recently for a tetanus booster.

I have a girlfriend, whom I adore, but I'm never tempted to eat at her place as her plates are forever piled up in the sink like the Leaning Tower of Pisa and the air is filled with the aroma of soiled cat litter. It's like a student house with cats. This same girlfriend wonders why every time she asks potential new boyfriends home, she rarely sees them again.

'If your kitchen is growing cobwebs, chances are your social life is too.' ♥

Your kitchen is the beating heart of your home. It makes a statement to the world about who you are and whether you are expecting company. A pantry bereft of signs of life and a fridge full of penicillin colonies and half-eaten TV dinners is not good for your state of mind, let alone your social life. It's time you turned your pantry into a passport to popularity and your fridge into a social force. They are the front lines in your quest to become a cocktail-party queen.

In order to transform yourself into a kitchen vixen you will need to undertake a culinary makeover. It can be scary making those first few tentative steps into new terrain, so enlist a food-savvy friend to help you rethink your relationship with your kitchen. Make sure they have some culinary know-how or it may end up being a case of the blonde leading the blonde. Recruiting a sympathetic friend will make the whole exercise far speedier and also means you get to enjoy some fun and free therapy along the way. Make sure you have some Chardonnay or other fortifying brew on hand and some snacks to share as you tackle your kitchen transformation.

The first place to start is with a spring clean. This can be daunting for us housework-avoidant harlots, but think of it as a cathartic exercise. You are dusting the cobwebs from your social life. Get rid of clutter so you have some clear surfaces to work with and then banish any residual dirt and debris in readiness to do an inventory of your culinary resources.

Prettify Your Pantry

The first step is to take the shoes out of the stove and stop using it for storage. In fact, pull everything out of the cupboards and fridge. Look at all the use-by dates on all your products. Unlike sexy chicks and vintage wines, foodstuffs don't improve with age. Throw out anything old and past its expiration date and leave the rest standing so you and your friend can sort through what you have and don't have.

Cupboards that are so messy you need a satellite navigation system to find anything aren't conducive to cooking. Get your friend to help you prettify your pantry and feng shui your fridge.

As you do so, consult the list of staples and standbys provided overleaf, checking off the items you have and making a wish list of the things you're sure to need. You can also make a note of any equipment you are going to need on your kitchen wish list. Likewise, take an inventory of your glasses, platters and other partyware.

Staples: As Important as Good Underwear

It doesn't matter what you wear if your boobs are knocking around your knees or your underwear is riding up your derrière. You need the right clothing basics to make an outfit work. It's the same with your kitchen. You need a collection of staples, like frozen puff pastry and Cheddar cheese, to enable you to whip up some fabulous finger food at a moment's notice.

Much like with your wardrobe, it's important to have a core culinary style rather than trying out every new food fad, which will only leave you stocked with a bunch of expensive, mismatching products and nothing to eat. With the recipes in this book, I have kept it simple and stuck to easy versions of the classics. Like a little black dress and a pair of heels, they will never go out of style. When you have the right basics, you will see how easy it is to throw a party menu together.

LIKE SEXY UNDERWEAR, FOOD STAPLES BOLSTER A GOOD DISH. HERE IS A LIST OF THINGS YOU SHOULD ALWAYS HAVE ON HAND.

Wine

No lazy hostess cooks without this divine liquid. And sometimes we even add it to the food.

Condiments & Spices

Salt

Pepper

Cayenne

Chilli sauce

East End Fish Seasoning

Paprika

Basics

Coffee, regular and decaf

Tea

Olive oil

Vegetable oil

Balsamic vinegar

Dijon mustard

Mayonnaise

Barbecue sauce

Buffalo Wings sauce

Worcestershire sauce

Plain flour

Italian seasoning

Marinara sauce

Ketchup

Tabasco sauce

Tomato juice

Aerosol whipped cream

Parchment paper

Aluminium foil

Cling film

TIP: Buy mild, low-salt crackers. Flavoured crackers can be too over-powering to serve with cheese and dips. I like Ritz Crackers but any variety will work.

TIP: Sour cream is perfect for combining with packet soup mixes to create instant dips.

Canned & Dried Goods

Packet of onion soup mix
Can of mushroom pieces
Jar of jalapeño peppers

Snacks

Cheesy breadsticks
Potato crisps
Nuts, salted and roasted
Party Snack Mix
Popcorn
Crackers
Dried dates, apricots or figs

Sweet Stuff

Granulated sugar
Brown sugar
Honey
Maple syrup
Apricot jam
Semi-sweet cooking chocolate

Fridge

Sour cream
Parmesan cheese
Grated mozzarella cheese
Cheddar cheese

Milk
Cream

Freezer

Streaky bacon
Frozen meatballs
Cocktail sausages
Potato wedges
Frozen puff pastry
(Make sure you put a date on any foodstuffs you put in the freezer.)

Perishables

I wouldn't worry about buying perishables until just before the party.

TIP: Put onions and potatoes in the fridge for a longer shelf life. And keep bacon in the freezer if you aren't using it straight away.

Equip Your Kitchen

Take an inventory of your kitchen equipment, crockery and stemware and see if you need to supplement. You will need a supply of wine glasses and cocktail glasses as well as tumblers for mixed drinks and beer. You can also never have enough small plates. Ditto for napkins. It's always wise to have some paper or plastic plates and glasses on hand for when you have a larger party.

If you're on a tight budget, then find a discount houseware outlet or check eBay for deals. You can also buy inexpensive glasses and crockery at discount stores. Small bowls for dips and assorted nibbles are also essential. And, if you like, get some cheese knives if you want to be fancy. Otherwise, regular ones will do.

Charity shops also often have a selection of wine, champagne and cocktail glasses, as well as silver serving trays. Vintage pieces will also give your party a dash of retro glam. Don't worry about getting things that go together. Eclectic table settings are interesting and fun.

Equipment

**THIS LIST OF EQUIPMENT SHOULD SEE
YOU THROUGH A COCKTAIL PARTY. BUILD IT
ITEM BY ITEM WITH YOUR WISH LIST.**

- Wine rack (not essential but very handy)
- Bottle openers
- Cork stoppers (in case there is some leftover quaffable wine)
- Tumblers, cocktail glasses and wine glasses (plastic glasses as a back-up are a good idea too)
- Cocktail napkins
- Liquid measuring jug
- Cocktail shaker
- Pitchers for bulk cocktails
- An ice bucket or two
- Ice trays
- An ice box (you can also fill a bath with ice to put extra alcohol in)
- A blender for frozen cocktails
- Ice tongs
- Platters for serving
- Small plates for eating off (or just dine from napkins)
- Microwave-safe plates for heating
- Small bowls for nibbles
- Cheese knives (not necessary but nice to have)
- A basic supply of cutlery
- Coffee cups and teaspoons
- Sugar bowl and small milk jug
- Cutting boards (one for meat and one for veggies)
- Measuring cups
- Nested measuring spoons
- 2 rimmed baking trays
- 1 small and 1 large frying pan (preferably non-stick)
- 1 small, 1 medium and 1 large saucepan (preferably non-stick)
- Kitchen tongs
- Serrated knife (for bread, etc.)
- Good, sharp chef's knife
- Pastry brush (for putting oil on crostinis, or just drizzle it)

- Wooden spoons
- Spatula
- Box grater
- Can opener
- Whisk
- Food processor
- Food strainer

- Mixing bowls in different sizes
- 24-cup mini-muffin tin
- Pizza pans
- Airtight storage containers
- Kitchen mitts
- Kitchen towels
- Sexy apron

Wish Lists for Deserving Divas

I suggest you put your wish list on Amazon and make it public so your friends can consult it for present ideas. You can even call it something imaginative like 'My Heavenly Kitchen' or 'Cocktail Dreams' or 'Help! Save Me from Paper Plates'. This way you can kill two birds with one stone: stop your friends from giving you any more of the useless presents and trinkets they foist on you for Christmas and birthdays and gradually build your kitchen and cocktail arsenal, ready for a nuclear assault on your social sphere. All without costing you an extra penny.

Think about it: they have bridal registries, why not bachelorette registries? Those brides get all the goodies, but Bridezilla and her big day shouldn't eclipse us single sisters. Lord knows no one would ever get married if it wasn't for our endless counselling and cocktail-pouring. They should be giving us gifts (not to mention a medal) for finally seeing them down the aisle. Singletons need homewares too. In fact, more so as we don't have hubby to fork out for most of the stuff.

Don't forget that many people also bring hostess gifts. Send guests to your wish list too. Every housewarming party or impromptu soirée is an opportunity to make a subtle suggestion about what you could use to build your dream kitchen or cocktail bar. Ultimately, building your kitchen supplies is a selfless gesture. You only want these things in order to make happy hour even happier for your friends. These are the gifts that keep on giving. Honestly, if you were any nicer, you would have to come with an insulin injection.

The Camp Cook's One-Pot Dinner Party

If you can imagine a gay version of Crocodile Dundee, only wielding a saucepan rather than a Bowie knife, then you can picture my Australian friend Phil. This outback adventurer loves exploring the desert and making delicious campfire meals.

If you have so little equipment you may as well be camping, Phil's 'Lentils in Limbo' opposite is ideal. While not a cocktail-party dish, it's ideal for a nosh-up with friends.

One-Pot
RECIPE

To make this recipe all you will need is a bottle opener, can opener, knife and a large saucepan.

splash of olive oil
1 onion, diced
2 garlic cloves, minced
1 large jalapeño chilli pepper, de-seeded and diced
1 dried chorizo sausage, sliced
60ml red wine
2 medium potatoes, diced
2 carrots, diced
500ml water
2 tbsp tomato paste
½ tsp salt and ¼ tsp pepper
2 x 390g cans lentils

Fry the onion, garlic and chilli in the oil until soft. Add sliced chorizo and continue to cook for a couple of minutes before adding the red wine. Cook until the wine has almost evaporated, then add potatoes, carrots, half the water, tomato paste, and salt and pepper. Bring this lot to the boil. Then add drained lentils and remaining water. Return to the boil and then turn down the heat and simmer for about 15 minutes, until you get a very thick soup. Phil recommends serving this dish with crusty bread and butter.

TIP: FOR EXTRA HEAT, YOU CAN LEAVE THE SEEDS IN THE PEPPER.

Pizza Dinner Party

Hosting a pizza party is about the easiest thing you can do and it involves very little equipment, expenditure or effort. All you need is a couple of pizza pans. Or you can use a baking tray – just make your pizzas rectangular to fit. If you want to get fancy, buy a pizza cutter to slice them, or your kitchen knife will do. Beyond this, you will need a bunch of bowls for toppings, and napkins and paper plates. Shopping will take only minutes and you can even order the ingredients online.

All you need is some ready-made pizza bases, or you can use puff pastry as a base. If you use puff pastry, roll the bases out on a lightly floured surface and fold the edges in about 1cm on each side to form a rim before putting them on a lightly greased baking tray.

Apart from dough, all you will need is marinara or pizza sauce, grated mozzarella cheese and a few toppings you think would be yummy, like pitted olives, sliced pepperoni, sautéed onions, ham, pineapple and mushrooms. You can also add other types of cheese like goat's cheese or Parmesan.

Encourage your friends to bring the toppings for their favourite pizza recipe to add to the options. They can put together their favourite combination for everyone to sample or they can experiment with different toppings. Take a poll later to see which flavour was the most popular.

Make sure any toppings that need cooking are pre-cooked so it's just a case of heating them up. Before your guests arrive, preheat the oven so it's as hot as Hades

'Pizza is a lot like sex. When its good, it's really good. When its bad, its still pretty good.' ♥

(about 250°C). Put the pizza bases or rolled-out pastry on the table, along with the sauce, mozzarella and toppings for your guests to assemble their own. Then cook according to packet instructions. A pizza party gets everyone participating. This has two advantages: there is barely any work for you and guests can't really complain about something they assembled.

PIZZA FIT FOR A QUEEN: The first Margherita pizza was made by a Neapolitan chef called Raffaele Esposito to honour the visit of the Queen Consort of Italy, Margherita of Savoy. He created this pizza topped with tomatoes, mozzarella and basil to represent the colours of the Italian flag. It was history in the making.

Plan Your Party

PREPARATION IS KEY.
*If you organize everything in advance,
then you can conserve your energy for
consuming cocktails.*

*I*f you've only just become reacquainted with your pantry, then you will probably want to plan your first party well in advance to avoid unecessary angst. But that doesn't mean it has to feel like work. Planning presents as much of an opportunity to socialize as the night itself. It's a great chance to bond with friends and have fun plotting while imbibing inspirational cocktails. Until then, here is a timeline for planning your first foray into cocktail-party infamy.

One Month Before

DECIDE ON A PARTY THEME

The best way to start is to gather together some of your girlfriends to test-drive libations and decide on your signature sip. After you agree on the ideal cocktail, selecting the theme is easy. I also find that a few medicinal beverages really frees up my thinking process. After you agree on the cocktail and theme, you can brainstorm other elements with your friends, as well as begin delegating tasks to them.

SELECT SOME SEXY THREADS

A party is really just an excuse to put on your glad rags, so picking the right outfit is key. Find a set of threads you feel fabulous in and then make sure you have all the elements you need to pull it together, from bling to belts to beautiful hosiery. Leading ladies have dress rehearsals and so should you: try on the entire outfit well before the party to see how it looks. Again, it can be a good idea to invite a friend over to give you feedback (over more cocktails, of course). You can also start planning your hair and make-up. It's worth

*Leading ladies have dress rehearsals and so should **YOU**.* ♥

spending the time to rethink your image before re-launching yourself on the party circuit. Think of it as You 2.0.

Three Weeks Before

THE GUEST LIST

Put together your guest list of friends and new acquaintances. Cocktail parties are an opportunity to mix old and new. So invite some of the usual suspects but also ask along some fresh faces – people you don't know so well but are intrigued by. Invite a few extra friends in case people drop out at the last moment. I have friends who would go to the opening of a packet of crisps who I can always count on to make up the numbers.

SEND OUT THE INVITES

Download one of the irresistible invitations on my website at babescott.com and personalize it with your party details. Send it out about three weeks in advance. Ask your guests to RSVP at least a week ahead so you have time to organize some ringarounds if too many can't attend. Ask a few guests to bring an interesting single friend if you need to make up the numbers.

Two Weeks Before

A MENU FOR MINXES

Decide on the menu and recruit your sous chef. They will be the wind beneath your culinary wings. Get together to discuss the easy, enticing menus in this book. If you haven't conquered your kitchen yet, then get him or her to help you lead the charge.

Plan the finger-food menu and create a shopping list. Separate the list into perishables and non-perishables and buy all the latter in advance. Make any dishes that can be frozen to give you a head start. Your faithful sous chef can also help you work out the amount of alcohol you will need and what you will buy versus what you will ask friends to bring.

TOE-TAPPING TUNES

Some mood-enhancing soundtracks are essential. I have recommended tunes for every occasion for you to download at babescott.com. If you have friends with a great music collection, then flatter and cajole them into creating a special playlist for the evening. This will help you add to your own collection.

One Week Before

ASSEMBLE YOUR PARTY ARSENAL

Make sure you have all the equipment you will need to cook, plus enough serving platters, pitchers and glasses. Prepare a complete checklist and beg, borrow or steal what you don't have. And make sure to have paper plates, plastic cups and paper towels on hand in case you run out of crockery, glassware or napkins. Think about the decorations, and print any personalized placemats you want to use and laminate them to use on your platters.

Two Days Before

SHOPPING AND COOKING

Buy the perishables a day or two ahead so you now have all the ingredients you need. Prepare as much as you can the day before with your trusty sous chef and do the rest the morning of the party. Buy the alcohol in advance and make sure you have all your bar supplies and you've frozen plenty of ice.

The Day

Do whatever last-minute assembly and cooking on the morning of the party and prepare a few pitchers of your signature cocktail if you haven't done it already. Then spend the afternoon relaxing and getting ready. Make sure your sous chef arrives early, in time for a pre-party cocktail and to help do all the last-minute assembling. Then put on your soundtrack and your biggest smile and let the world in.

As Her Royal Hostess and the Queen of festivities

you need to look and feel your REGAL best.

Here are some tips to make sure you shine like
a supernova at your next soirée.

4

Queenly
Comportment

Primping and Preening

The hostess should feel fabulous when she greets her guests rather than ready to reach for an industrial-sized Anadin. Read on for advice on how to get in the mood for a marvellous evening.

A queen should be in full spirits rather than unduly stressed when she greets her guests. This is why you should do everything in your power to take the angst out of your entertaining efforts and leave plenty of time to primp and preen before the party. As Hilda on *Ugly Betty* said: 'Fabulous doesn't just happen.' Like every leading lady, you need time to pamper yourself before you greet your adoring public. Cleopatra never spent the day stressing before a banquet. Instead she took milk baths and had massages. Likewise, Hollywood stars don't spend the day scrubbing the sink before they hit the red carpet. They spend it

getting fussed over rather than fussing. Similarly, spend the day of your event preparing to play the siren.

Turn your home into a mini-spa for the day. Make yourself feel beautiful from the top of your elegantly coiffed head to the tips of your manicured toes. Follow the example of Oscar Wilde, who once said: 'To love oneself is the beginning of a lifelong romance.' If you feel loved up, it's easy to bestow your good cheer on others. Don't be shy about recruiting a hair- and make-up-savvy friend to help you feel your best. Every queen has an entourage of helpers. It's all about tapping the talents of your social circle. Here are a few suggestions to help you relax and get ready for your big night.

A Bubble Bath

There is nothing as sensual as a bubble bath to get you in the mood, particularly if you have a Man Friday to help you lather up. Even if you don't have a doting male attendant, you can romance yourself by lighting some tea-light candles and making yourself a dresser cocktail to sip as you luxuriate. A Mimosa is the perfect pre-party mood enhancer, but anything with sparkling wine will help you unwind. I love adding a little rose oil to the bath water to give it a delicious scent. You can even add real rose petals if you have any handy.

You can make an easy exfoliant by mixing olive oil with either

salt or sugar and giving your skin a good scrub to make it silky smooth. Don't forget to shave – there's nothing sexy about looking like a yeti and you never know who might be caressing your legs later. Make sure you moisturize your body after you towel dry. For an easy homemade moisturizer, mix olive oil with a little rose oil or any other essential oil. Remember, you are only as old as your skincare regime!

Preen Like a Princess

If you have the bucks, by all means go out and get a mani-pedi from your local nail guru. Otherwise, you can easily do it yourself at home. There is nothing less alluring than toes that look like they belong in a museum. A retina-rupturing red shade for fingers and toes is classic Hollywood. Don't be in a rush. Spend the time doing your nails the way they do in the nail salon. Clean, file and wage war on those cuticles. Make sure to moisturize and then put on a base coat, two coats of polish and a top-coat. Then dry them with a hairdryer.

Then it's time to move on to your mane. If your hair feels lustrous so will you. Go to the salon if you have time and cash to spare. Otherwise, give yourself a blow-dry or get a glamorous friend to do it for you and catch up on all the gossip while she helps you get gorgeous. If you want to try an up-do or something befitting your style icon, there are plenty of clips on YouTube that show you how to create any hairstyle from a French twist to the vintage Victory Roll. I also have a tutorial on my website that shows you the secrets to creating my own fabulous up-do. Check it out on the book page of my website at babescott.com.

When you're finished, spritz some sexy perfume on your hair, your neck and wrists. A queen should smell good enough to eat.

Make-up Minx

I personally love classic pin-up make-up. It's glamorous and easy to achieve. You can also emulate the look of your favourite fashion icon and just add your own twist.

If you aren't confident you can put the HO into Hollywood, then consider getting a makeover at your local beauty emporium.

Most make-up departments will do this free if you buy a product or two. So wait till you need to replenish your beauty supplies and book an appointment. Take along a picture of the look you want to recreate as well as the make-up you already have so you don't double up. If you want to save money, buy similar products to the ones the consultant used to create your look in the beauty aisle of your local chemist. It's a cinch to colour-match cosmetics.

You can also ask a style-savvy friend to help you, or look at some how-to videos on YouTube. Better still, check out the make-up tutorial on my website, which will show you how to become a minx in minutes.

Make sure you practise before your big event and that you have the look nailed. You don't want to greet your guests looking like you put on your make-up with a crayon. With a little patience and practice you will be able to create your perfect party face.

Now crank up the soundtrack and wait for the party to begin.

TOO-SEXY SOUNDTRACK: I'VE CREATED THE PERFECT PLAYLIST TO MAKE YOU FEEL LIKE A SIREN. THESE SONGS ARE SO SEXY THEY WILL MAKE YOU GO UP A CUP SIZE. GO TO BABESCOTT. COM TO FIND THIS POUT-WORTHY PLAYLIST.

Dress to Thrill

The first rule of regality is to work out the right party outfit. It's your moment in the spotlight and you need to shine. Here are some tips on dressing to dazzle.

$\mathcal{E}$ntertaining is all about playing the siren. The hostess should be the hottest dish to come out of the kitchen. As such, fashion should be the first item on the menu. It's your chance to dazzle. And while you can be slothful at the stove top, it doesn't do to be slovenly when it comes to looking your sexy best. This is your opportunity to enjoy the spotlight and embrace your inner minx. It's about having your own Oscar-worthy fashion moment.

Queens set a high standard when it comes to glamour, so let your guests know there is a dress code and if they don't pass muster they won't get past the velvet rope. If they aren't prepared to dress with a bit of pizzazz, they can stay put at home and eat peanut butter out of the jar. The late fashion icon Diana Vreeland once declared: 'I don't hate bad taste. I just hate no taste.' I tend to agree. I don't care if my guests dress in drag or come as the White Witch from Narnia, as long as they make an effort.

My parties generally inspire so many outlandish outfits they resemble the bar scene from *Star Wars*. I have a petite male friend who likes to dress as Super Mario and my Elvis-impersonator friend always adds a touch of Graceland. There are also usually more sequins than you would see at a Shirley Bassey tribute.

However, it's the hostess who truly sets the tone. Imagine if the compère for the Emmys turned up in a sweatshirt and an old pair of jeans. The whole night would lose its lustre. Similarly, it's key that you make sure your outfit sizzles. Here are some tips to putting on the ritz.

Find a Style Inspiration

The best way to gain style inspiration is to find a role model. Look at movies, magazines and TV shows to find a fashion muse who inspires you with their dress sense. I personally don't think you can go past the fashion icons of Hollywood's Golden Era. These gals really knew how to turn on the glamour as well as enjoy a good time. For instance, look to the original blonde bombshells Marilyn Monroe and Jayne Mansfield, or the bewitching brunettes Ava Gardner and Audrey Hepburn. These women were walking exclamation marks who commanded the spotlight. My own look I often describe as 'Audrey Hepburn on steroids'.

Once you find a fashion diva you would like to emulate, start channelling some of her fashion moxie. Start a 'look book' or scrapbook of images of your muse for sartorial inspiration. Watch her movies and study her every nuance. In this way, you will start to absorb some of her style sensibility. When you try something on, ask yourself: 'What would Marilyn think?' Or pose this question to whomever your fashion mentor is (just try not to do this aloud in front of any shop assistants). Soon you will be channelling your muse better than a Ouija board.

'It's better to be looked over than overlooked.'
– Mae West ❤

Flaunt Your Assets

Dressing like a siren is all about playing up your curves. Again, look to the bombshells of yesteryear. They weren't frightened to flaunt their wares in figure-hugging outfits. Elizabeth Taylor was famously sewn into her slip dress in *BUtterfield 8* and most of Marilyn's dresses were tighter than a tourniquet. You can create the illusion of an hourglass figure even if you are as straight up and down as a swizzle stick. As Sophia Loren once said: 'Sex appeal is fifty per cent what you've got and fifty per cent what people think you've got.'

Flaunt your assets and play down your figure flaws. For instance, if you have a devastating cleavage then by all means put it on display. If you have great pins, then play them up with a slit skirt or a hemline shorter than The Situation's attention span. By the same token, play down the parts you don't want to bring attention to. For instance, big hips and bubble skirts are as incompatible as Donald Trump and Rosie O'Donnell. In fact, I think bubble skirts should be banned – or only sold over the counter in chemists' as an alternative contraception.

And I wouldn't suggest wearing anything that exposes your midriff unless you have abs like Britney Spears and don't intend eating anything. I personally don't wear anything I can't put shapewear underneath. In my case, creating curves is all about the art of fat redistribution.

The Oscar-worthy Outfit

Once you know your style icon, finding the perfect party frock should be relatively easy. Gather an image or two of your favourite femme fatale in an outfit you would love to wear and look for something similar. If you need reassurance, ask a stylish friend to help you shop to give you a second opinion and encourage you to embrace your inner diva.

Remember, you can get things altered as long as they have the basics (sort of like remoulding boyfriends). You can alter the hemline, shorten the sleeves or even add a split. I have my local tailor create sweetheart necklines on almost all my frocks. These darling necklines really flatter the bustline. Making a subtle tweak is also a great way of adding a little of your own twist of lemon to every outfit.

'It's simple. I believe in pink. I believe in wearing lipstick. I believe happy girls are the prettiest girls. I believe in miracles.'
— Audrey Hepburn ❤

I also often add a cameo or a diamante brooch to the neckline of my frock. These type of retro glam trinkets are easy and inexpensive to find in vintage shops and lend a little sparkle. Little touches like this are like adding a garnish to a great dish.

I love to finish my hostess ensemble with a saucy apron – something more along the lines of a French maid than a matronly smock. If you want to be an apron provocateur, there are plenty of pin-up-worthy pinafores to be found online or on eBay that will make you feel like a kitchen vixen.

Curve-enhancing Underwear

Cleavage is one of the key weapons in every woman's charm arsenal. Take a cue from Nigella Lawson, as famous for her cup size as she is for her cupcakes. Investing in a gravity-defying bra is essential. If you are small-chested, a push-up bra with a little extra padding can perform miracles. If you are well endowed in the mammary department, then get the scaffolding you need to hoist the girls up so they are perkier than an eighteen-year-old cheerleader. Once you've got the twin turrets in position, then you can show off your décolletage with a sexy neckline or form-fitting frock.

Apart from a decent bra, you will need quality shapewear unless you are one of those naturally skinny people we all envy. But for those of us who have no self-discipline when it comes to second helpings, Spanx is our new best friend. This figure-sculpting underwear is the secret weapon for many leading ladies, from Katy Perry to Gwyneth Paltrow. This miracle undergarment is the best invention since the space shuttle, only more practical.

Smoking-hot Heels

No party outfit is complete without a pair of heels. When was the last time you saw Beyoncé saunter onstage wearing Hush Puppies? She would wear stilettos if both legs were in a cast. Flat shoes are the visual equivalent of Valium. Even if you find it hard to wear stilettos, there are other options. For instance, kitten heels are adorable and easy on the feet, while wedge heels are very wearable yet can be wicked-looking.

My friend Peekaboo Pointe, a stripper (and stove-top siren) who has strutted her stuff across the States, recommends platforms for heels you can shimmy in all night long. The extra support in the toe area makes them more comfortable than regular stilettos. Peekaboo swears by the Pleaser brand, but there are plenty of other sexy shoe labels showcasing platforms that are easy on the pocketbook. As Marilyn Monroe once said: 'Give a girl the right shoes and she can conquer the world.'

Badass Bling

A bit of bling goes a long way. I think jewellery should accent your outfit, not take it over. You don't want to look like a Christmas tree or have someone mistake your earrings for light fixtures. Find a key piece that brings your outfit to life, like a beautiful pair of earrings or a simple strand of faux pearls. Once you find your statement piece, make sure any other jewellery you wear complements it. I also love a tiara. They always make me feel like a queen.

Belts are a great way to cinch a waist and help create the illusion of an hourglass shape. A faux fur stole can zhush up any fashion ensemble. Hosiery really adds some sex appeal to an outfit. It also makes your pins look a whole lot smoother. Sheer tights work fine, but if you really want to sex up your outfit try foxy fishnets or stockings with garters. And if you want to add some retro flair, seamed stockings also look très elegant. I know girls who draw a seam up their legs with a marker pen and put their tights on top. If you try this trick, make sure whoever draws on your seams hasn't had too many cocktails and can manage a straight line. Ditto for when you walk your own red carpet to greet your guests looking like a star.

One of the easiest ways to entertain is to host a cocktail party. It's a fabulous way to ...

... *win friends under the influence.*

5

Bring Back

Cocktail

Hour

Host Happy Hour at Home

Everyone with a pulse and a palate likes happy hour. Turn your lounge into an impromptu cocktail bar and invite your friends over for a celebratory drink.

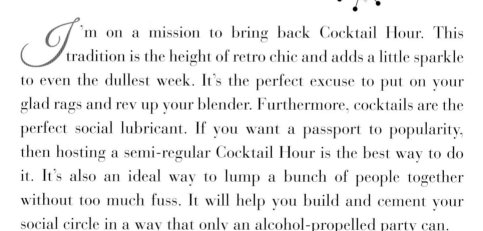

I'm on a mission to bring back Cocktail Hour. This tradition is the height of retro chic and adds a little sparkle to even the dullest week. It's the perfect excuse to put on your glad rags and rev up your blender. Furthermore, cocktails are the perfect social lubricant. If you want a passport to popularity, then hosting a semi-regular Cocktail Hour is the best way to do it. It's also an ideal way to lump a bunch of people together without too much fuss. It will help you build and cement your social circle in a way that only an alcohol-propelled party can.

Cocktail culture really started in the 1920s. In the 1950s, the cocktail became an even greater emblem of sophistication. The

at-home cocktail party was super-fashionable and Cocktail Hour in bars began to embrace lounge acts, burlesque and music.

Hollywood also embraced the glamour of the cocktail. It would be hard to recognize any Golden-Era bombshells without a cocktail in hand. In *The Seven Year Itch*, Marilyn Monroe dunks potato crisps in champagne and in the 1932 classic, *Red Dust*, Clark Gable chats up Jean Harlow with the line, 'Mind if I get drunk with you?'. Humphrey Bogart, the greatest of all screen gangsters, once said: 'If everyone in the world would take three drinks, we would have no trouble.'

The modern-day Cocktail Hour is not just a nod to the Golden Era of Hollywood and the Roaring Twenties, but a way to resurrect glamour. Cocktail Hour presents a chance to elevate ourselves above the mundane and find a little magic in a glass. Essentially, Cocktail Hour is drinky-poos with a dress code. It's a get-together with friends, neighbours and any other stray socialite you want to invite to raise a toast (and get toasted) *in style*.

Cocktail Hour can be a fairly intimate affair or a big, thrashing, swinging-from-the-chandeliers event. It's an opportunity to quaff cocktails and snack on finger food while mingling with other guests. In theory, cocktail parties go from two to three hours. However, my soirées usually last long into the night. On my invitation I generally put a start and end time of 7 p.m. to 9 p.m., but I'm nearly always trying to crowbar the laggards out the door at well past midnight. See my tips on 'Getting Guests to Go Home on pages 224–5' if you need help ejecting your guests when the festivities are over.

'Cocktail Hour is a way to **RESURRECT** *glamour.'* ❤

I recommend starting at 7 p.m., as cocktail parties are meant to kick off early. They are civilized affairs rather than the sort of open-house party you roll up to when the pubs close. This also gives your friends time to have a light supper beforehand, or at least pour themselves a bowl of Weetabix. On that note, make sure you let them know that it's not a fully fledged dinner so they can scoff something in advance and don't arrive completely famished.

Since there are bound to be a couple of last-minute no-shows, invite one extra person for every ten guests who say they are coming. Make sure your friends also know you are not Ivana-be-rich Trump and to bring a bottle of plonk. Work out what you need and let each of your guests bring a contribution to the beverage quota. Remember: the purpose of this event is to up your fun quotient, not to land you in the 'pour' house.

Read on for some suggestions for making your happy hour even happier.

A Sinfully Sexy Invitation

It's worth emailing a proper invitation. Simply calling on the phone or sending a random text doesn't convey a sense of occasion. Nor do the generic invitations you can find online. A gorgeous invitation will make your event stand out and will also convey the right mood. The invitation should evoke old-school glamour and a sense of excitement. It should also clearly set a dress code. You want your friends to know they can't just turn up in their flip-flops for a beer but should do their best to look foxy.

For this precise reason, we have created suitably glamorous invitations you can download from my website, which convey exactly the right style with a little dash of sin. You can take the design and personalize it to print or email from your computer. Simply go to my website at babescott.com and look for Invitations under the book tab to find them.

It's Raining Men

One of the key ingredients to a great party is a fair representation of the opposite sex. What's a party without some frisson and flirting? Answer: it's a PTA meeting with vodka. (Boring!) We've all been to gatherings where the testosterone-to-oestrogen ratio is so askew that you feel as if you are sipping Cosmopolitans on Cheerleader Island. It's important to have enough single guys on hand to get the pheromones flying.

There are a couple of ways to boost the testosterone ratio. One is to actively go out man-hunting for hunky guys to ask to your party. Make this a mission when you next go out with your girlfriends. You can also go through your own Rolodex of amours past and recycle your leftover loves. The other trick is to tell your girlfriends that their price of entry is to bring an eligible single man, preferably one you've never met. Rather than calling these 'singles parties', which can create too much social pressure (the term can induce a facial tic in most men), I call these 'One Degree of Separation Parties'. Your girlfriends will have to raid their social closet to find an eligible guy you don't know, adding an element of surprise to the event. The mix of old and new friends adds electricity. It also takes the pressure off you having to be the man-wrangler finding all the eligible men to invite, and makes the whole night more interesting and turns it into a participation sport.

Over-thirty Lighting

Lighting is key to creating a romantic mood or the ambience of an old Hollywood film. Nothing flatters the complexion more than dim lighting (I call it 'over-thirty lighting'), which gives everyone an instant facelift. Use dimmers if you have them on ceiling lights. Otherwise, use lamps to create a soft glow. If you don't have dimmers, then consider getting some black or black-

and-white paper lanterns. These are a cheap solution for creating softer lighting.

Candles also add a sense of mystery. Just be careful where you place them so they aren't likely to be knocked over by careless revellers. I use tea lights in shot glasses as they are inexpensive and easy to replace. It's also nice to have a scented candle in the bathroom. Try and keep the lighting low in here too. While you don't want your guests to be doing their ablutions by Braille, you also don't want them to be overly lit. It really deflates the mood.

Spruce Up Your Space

Arrange furniture so that guests can move around the room easily and engage in a little impromptu dancing later on in the evening. Clear debris from whatever surfaces you can so guests have somewhere to leave their glasses and you have somewhere to put snack bowls. Make sure your guests can clearly see the snacks and offer them to people when you're doing the rounds.

'Dress up trays and platters with photos of friends or some DELICIOUS Man Candy.' ❤

Set up a table for beverages, as well as a separate station for finger food. Preferably, position these stations on opposite sides of the room to cut down on people traffic. Make sure there is some seating around the sides of the room for guests who need to catch their breath from dancing like the possessed.

Throw a couple of tablecloths over your stations to spruce them up. Put one or two citrus-fruit halves, cut side down, on the table for people to stick their used toothpicks into. If you don't have enough serving plates, then improvise – cutting boards, picture frames, lightweight mirrors or even large books. You can also often buy beautiful vintage platters and serving plates from antique stores for next to nothing.

Decorative Touches

Decorate with some festive bunches of flowers if you like, even if you borrow them from the garden of a green-fingered neighbour. Vine leaves also work a treat and create a Bacchanalian effect. If you are an artsy-craftsy type and want to save money, consider creating vases out of old bottles by purchasing a bottle cutter. Or you could put a handy friend to the task. You can also make votive candleholders and even drinking glasses.

The best way to dress up trays and platters is with photos of friends or some delicious Man Candy. All you have to do is print out photos and laminate them. Then *Voila!* Instant placemats. You can either use funny pictures of friends or download one or more of the 'Eat Off His Abs' photos from my website at babescott. com. Look under the Man Candy tab to find placemat-sized photos of totally edible guys. These placemats protect your platters from spillage and are great conversation starters. If you have any random things to give away, you could even start an informal caption competition.

Encourage Self-service

It's important to plan the night so you don't spend it surgically attached to your shaker or blender. That's why I've given you pitcher recipes for all of the signature drinks you can pre-prepare in pitchers before guests arrive. While some purists would tell you to pour to order, trust me that your guests will guzzle these pitchers as if it was Prohibition all over again. Back in Don Draper's day, savvy hostesses nearly always pre-made pitchers of their selected elixir because they knew they would be too pie-eyed to pour later. For pitcher recipes, see the following section on 'Signature Sips'.

After the first drink, make it clear that guests have to fend for themselves. Leave out your pitchers, as well as beer, wine and vodka. Preferably,

My Favourite Toast:
'I would rather be with you lot than the best people in the world.' ♥

have all the beverages arranged on ice in your makeshift bar. Leave out glasses, bottle openers and garnishes. Put any surplus alcohol that needs to chill in a bathtub filled with ice. Then pour yourself a drink and let everyone take care of themselves.

Smooth Soundtracks

Music helps your guests unwind and gets them into a celebratory mood. A great soundtrack is crucial for to a memorable night. The tunes selected should ideally match your theme and the atmosphere you want to create. The best way to manage the music is to create a couple of playlists for the party so you can strike the right mood. The earlier one can be a bit more mellow and then as things rev up put on a party mix.

To make it easy for you, I've compiled retro-inspired soundtracks for all the cocktail-party themes in the Signature Sip section, as well as a 'Dance Your Ass Off Party Mix' for when you want to amp up the evening. There is also a 'Sayonara Sweeties' soundtrack for the end of the night which will help you eject those friends who don't take the hint that it's time to go home. These playlists can also be found on my website at babescott.com.

'ALWAYS REMEMBER that I have taken more out of alcohol than alcohol has taken out of me.'

– Winston Churchill

Cocktail Hour

The signature sip is your

co-star for the night.

*Here are some suggestions to help
you select a concoction that complements
your dazzling personality.*

6

The Signature Sip

A cocktail party is not a cocktail party without a signature sip. You should select a potion that reflects your personality, works well as an icebreaker and has a 'wow' factor. I suggest you test-drive a few cocktails until you find one that puts you under its spell – an elixir that has that special *je ne sais quoi* and makes you fall in love at first sip. There are plenty of foolproof cocktail suggestions in this section to get you started on finding your 'soul mix'. I've focused on the classics, vintage cocktails that have lasted the test of time and put a slightly modern twist on them.

'*Select a potion that reflects your* **DAZZLING** *personality.*' ♥

A great cocktail doesn't need a dizzying list of ingredients. Just like the perfect frock, it needs little adornment. In my opinion, a cocktail should be simple. I would advise staying away from anything milky or creamy, or with more than four ingredients. Back in the 1950s and 60s, when cocktail parties were at their height, most drinks had few bells and whistles. They were perfect for Lazy Hostesses and, better still, most savvy (and slatternly) hostesses made them in pitchers. In the spirit of these sly sirens, all the cocktails I've selected can be pre-made in batches for easy serving. This way you won't have to spend the night stuck behind a blender or getting cocktail elbow from your shaker.

Frankly, there is no way I would trust my friends behind a bar even with the aid of a recipe taped to their wrist. Most of them can barely hold a cocktail and a conversation at the same time (and after a few beverages even this can be a struggle). Beyond this, your guests just want to let loose rather than have to test their wits with weights and measures. They would also likely end up putting in so much hard liquor that each drink could launch a moon rocket.

In some cases, I've altered the traditional recipes so they have a slightly lower alcohol quotient. You want your guests to get pleasantly soused rather than carried out on stretchers. It seems the Lazy Hostesses of yesteryear had titanium livers.

I've also altered some of the recipes to make them more affordable. For instance, in the 'Bubble Therapy' cocktail recipes I've substituted sparkling wine for champagne, which, in my opinion, is way over-inflated. Unless you are a modern-day Marie Antoinette, French fizz can send you into foreclosure. (The only French thing I'd fork out for when hosting a party is a manicure.) Remember, it's all about living a champagne lifestyle on a Budweiser budget. There are plenty of delicious sparkling wines you can buy for a fraction of the cost.

'Forego French fizz for sparkling wine. It's all about living a **CHAMPAGNE LIFESTYLE** *on a Budweiser budget.'* ❤

I've selected cocktails that have unisex appeal. I'd also keep this in mind if you mint your own drink. Or do two versions – one sweet and one with more machismo. No guy wants to be seen walking around with a pink Cosmopolitan covered in tiny umbrellas. You may as well tie his testicles in a slipknot. If you don't know a come-hither cocktail from a carburettor, get one of your male friends to sample your concoction and see if it makes him start speaking in a falsetto.

When dressing up your drinks, forget those tiny parasols or flower garnishes. Again, I return to the KISS principle: my refrain of Keeping It Simple Sister. A strawberry or a wedge of lemon, lime or orange can be easy yet stunning. You can even dispense with the garnishes altogether and decorate your drinks by simply serving them with one of your hundred-watt smiles.

Don't stress. Save your effort for flirting and making yourself look fabulous. It would be a sad state of affairs if your signature drink ends up better dressed than you.

Once you've decided what signature sip to serve, figure on providing two cocktails per guest for the first hour and one per guest for the following hours, making it three to four drinks per person over the course of the party. Calculate how much total alcohol you will need to buy or beg people to bring based on the amount of spirit required for each cocktail multiplied by the drinks you've estimated you will need. Once you know the number of guests, then you can pre-prepare the drinks as much as possible. Ideally, have your signature sip ready to hand to guests as they walk through the door and have the rest available for self-service pouring.

I would also have white and red wine on hand. Plan on roughly one bottle per two guests, though bear in mind that white wine tends to be more popular than red. I'd also suggest supplying some beer and vodka plus mixers like orange juice, cranberry juice and ginger ale, as well as soda water and tonic water. It's also worthwhile providing a couple of soft drinks like lemonade and Coca-Cola.

A PERSONAL
Twist

FEEL FREE TO ADD A PERSONAL TWIST to your selected elixir. It doesn't take much tampering to reinvent a tipple. The Gibson was created simply by some ingenious soul taking the olive out of the martini and putting a cocktail onion in. It may be a similarly tiny yet groundbreaking change for you to mint your own cocktail. For instance, try substituting a garnish, varying quantities or putting in a different juice, liqueur or other ingredient. You can even try adding a herb or spice, like cayenne or pepper, or giving it some heat by adding jalapeño.

Feel free to mint a new name for your cocktail, whether you give it a special twist or not. For instance, you could add a dash of irony by calling it the 'Fake Orgasm' (possibly host a competition for the best fake orgasm and give away a batch of this naughty cocktail as the prize). Or call your signature sip something suggestive like 'A Good Spanking'. This will help add a little frisson to the evening, especially when you ask your guests if they would like 'another Good Spanking', with a special inflection for the truly naughty boys. Creating names that would make your local barman blush is a fun activity to workshop with your girlfriends while you spend an afternoon test-driving cocktails together.

COCKTAIL QUEEN TIP: SHAKE IT BABY
William Powell in *The Thin Man* counselled the importance of rhythm when shaking a cocktail. He advised: 'A Manhattan you shake to foxtrot time, a Bronx to two-step time, but a dry martini you always shake to waltz time.' But you don't have to learn ballroom dancing to shake your drinks. Simply raise the shaker over your shoulder and shake hard for 10 to 15 seconds.

Bubble Therapy

There is nothing that starts a party better than a beverage with bubbles. If you select a sparkling-wine-based cocktail for your signature sip, I suggest theming the night to suit the faux champagne feeling. It's all about glamour in a glass, so put your best fashion foot forward. Try to evoke the effortless chic of Audrey Hepburn. If anyone embodies the sparkling stuff it's her delightful character Holly Golightly in the movie *Breakfast at Tiffany's.* She was the original style icon who scrimped to get by. Her best accessory was a champagne flute brimming with bubbles, and I'd be surprised if she didn't swap the French stuff for sparkling wine more often than not, considering she quaffed bubbles not only at dinner but for breakfast too.

'Being **AUDREY** *is the best cure for feeling ordinary.'* ❤

Ask your girlfriends to dress as Audrey. I believe being Audrey is the best cure for feeling 'ordinary' and isn't that what cocktail parties are all about? A simple shift dress, faux pearls, a tiara, high heels and an up-do and you will all be looking and feeling like Hollywood royalty. And what a great photo opportunity!

Make it easy for your male guests by asking them to dress like George Peppard or Cary Grant or one of Audrey's other elegant co-stars – or just tell them to put on a damn suit and retire the ripped jeans for a night. Even if they say they don't have one, they can beg, borrow or steal a nice set of threads from somewhere (if they want to be a slob they can stay at home and eat cereal out of a box).

If you have a cat that will stay put, drape it around your shoulders just like Audrey. It's more humane than a stole and your guests will just love patting your pussy.

As far as your abode goes, dim everything to get that flattering Vaseline-on-the-lens lighting they did in old Hollywood. Print out some images of Audrey and stick them around the place for inspiration. Perhaps put down some red carpet in your hallway and give your friends the paparazzi treatment by taking a photograph of them with their sparkling elixir as they walk through the door. It will be like hosting your own Oscars. Later on, you can all vote on the best dressed and give away a prize to the best Audrey. This could be as simple as a framed photograph of her with all the other Audreys. Ditto for your guys for the best Cary Grant. An oversized champagne glass also makes a great Audrey-inspired prize.

Before your sparkling soirée, make sure you watch *Breakfast at Tiffany's* to get you in the Audrey mood.

COCKTAIL QUEEN TIP: STIRRING NOT WHIRRING
Spirits are easily bruised, just like Taylor Swift, so stir them gently. Dunk your stirrer and twirl the shaft back and forth for 30 seconds.

Bubbly Beverages

Effervescent elixirs float away all our cares and put guests in a gay mood almost instantly. Sparkling wine was invented by a band of Benedictine monks who managed to ferment a path to heaven and is an incredibly versatile base for mixed drinks. I recommend using a 'Brut' sparkling wine because it's dryer than regular varieties and you don't want your signature sip to be too sweet.

All of these can be served in pitchers. You can mix all the ingredients apart from the fizzy stuff ahead of time. But it's best to wait to add the sparkling wine until just before the party starts or it will go flat. I've provided the quantities for a single cocktail as well as party-sized pours, along with an idea of the number of servings.

THE SECRET TO SIMPLE SYRUP: apart from your smile, you will need a sweetener for some of your elixirs. To make simple syrup, combine 225g white sugar with 250ml water. Bring to the boil over moderately high heat, stirring to dissolve sugar (about 3 minutes). Refrigerate in a sealed container.

BLUE
Velvet

**'I DON'T THINK I'VE EVER DRUNK CHAMPAGNE
BEFORE BREAKFAST BEFORE. WITH BREAKFAST ON
SEVERAL OCCASIONS, BUT NEVER BEFORE.'**

– George Peppard in *Breakfast at Tiffany's*.

*Audrey Hepburn would have loved this Tiffany Blue cocktail. It's the Hope
Diamond in a champagne flute.*

Single Serve

35ml (2 tbsp) blue Curaçao

Brut sparkling wine

Party Pitcher

220ml blue Curaçao

1 x 750ml bottle sparkling wine

Single serve: Pour blue Curaçao into a champagne flute and fill with sparkling
wine. Garnish with a strawberry or a maraschino cherry. The red looks gorgeous
against the Aegean blue.

Pitcher: Pour blue Curaçao into a pitcher and keep chilled in the fridge. Fill
with chilled sparkling wine and give a quick stir before the thirsty hordes arrive
so the fizz doesn't go flat. (About 6½ servings.)

THE
Redhead

'I DRINK TO MAKE MY FRIENDS MORE INTERESTING.'

– Don Marquis

This fiery drink has a reddish hue and the temperament to match. A couple of these cocktails and you will be feeling as frisky as a randy rabbit. Feel free to add a different liqueur to create your own drink if Chambord is not to your fancy. For instance, peach liqueur, red grapefruit liqueur, hibiscus liqueur . . . the list is endless. You could even add anise-flavoured Pernod for a variation on the classic 'Death in the Afternoon', or in this case 'Death in the Evening'.

Single Serve
18ml (3 tsp) Chambord
Brut sparkling wine

Party Pitcher
100ml Chambord
1 x 750ml bottle sparkling wine

Single serve: Pour the Chambord into the bottom of a champagne flute and fill with sparkling wine. Garnish with a raspberry or an impish smile.

Pitcher: Pour Chambord into the bottom of the pitcher and keep chilled in the fridge. Before the guests come fill the pitcher with the bottle of bubbly and stir sensuously. (About 5½ servings.)

TWIST: IF YOU RUN OUT OF THE SPARKLING STUFF, THEN YOU CAN MIX THE CHAMBORD WITH CHARDONNAY OR CHABLIS.

STORM IN A

D Cup

'HEY, DID YOU EVER TRY DUNKING POTATO CHIPS IN CHAMPAGNE BEFORE? IT'S REAL CRAZY.'

– Marilyn Monroe (as The Girl) in *The Seven Year Itch*

This is basically a Bellini made with sparkling wine rather than champagne. The Bellini was the preferred tipple of Mae West's character Peaches O'Day in the movie Every Day's a Holiday *and was originally crafted by Giuseppi Cipriani at Harry's Bar in Venice. It's a simple mixture of peach juice and sparkling wine and it has star quality. Feel free to substitute any other type of juice to mint your own luscious libation.*

Single Serve

35ml (2 tbsp) peach schnapps

Brut sparkling wine

Party Pitcher

220ml peach schnapps

1 x 750ml bottle sparkling wine

Single serve: Pour the peach schnapps into a champagne flute and fill wth sparkling wine. Garnish with a wink.

Pitcher: Pour peach schnapps into a pitcher and keep chilled in the fridge. Fill with the chilled sparkling wine and give a quick stir before the party gets started. (About 6½ servings.)

TWIST: YOU CAN MAKE THIS WITH PEACH NECTAR INSTEAD OF THE SCHNAPPS OR USE 70ML PEACH JUICE (SINGLE SERVE) INSTEAD OF THE SCHNAPPS. IF YOU WANT TO EXPERIMENT, TRY A DIFFERENT FLAVOUR OF SCHNAPPS.

THE BLONDE
Bombshell

**'GOOD GIRLS GO TO HEAVEN.
BAD GIRLS GO EVERYWHERE.'**

– Mae West

This bodacious beverage is the classic Hollywood champagne cocktail but with a cheap chic twist. We swapped the champagne for sparkling wine.

Single Serve

2 dashes Angostura bitters

1 tsp simple syrup (see p.87)

25ml (1 tbsp + 2 tsp) brandy

Brut sparkling wine

Party Pitcher

12 dashes Angostura bitters

8 tsp simple syrup (see p.87)

150ml brandy

1 x 750ml bottle sparkling wine

Single serve: Add the Angostura to the simple syrup in the bottom of the champagne flute, add brandy and fill with bubbly.

Pitcher: Put bitters and simple syrup in the bottom of the pitcher and stir gently. Pour in brandy and keep chilled in the fridge. Just before the party, fill with a bottle of chilled sparkling wine. Do your best Holly Golightly impersonation, air-kissing and laughing delightedly as you distribute your elixir. (About 6½ servings.)

SUGAR
Baby

'THE PROBLEM WITH PEOPLE WITH NO VICES IS THAT
GENERALLY YOU CAN BE PRETTY SURE THEY'RE GOING
TO HAVE SOME PRETTY ANNOYING VIRTUES.'

– Elizabeth Taylor

This twist on the classic Mimosa is a total crowd-pleaser. It's great for all ages and all seasons. It's like the Oprah of drinks – everyone loves it at any time of day.

Single Serve

15ml (1 tbsp) triple sec

45ml orange juice

Brut sparkling wine

Party Pitcher

120ml triple sec

360ml orange juice

1 x 750ml bottle sparkling wine

Single serve: Pour the triple sec and orange juice into a champagne flute and fill with sparkling wine.

Pitcher: Pour the triple sec and orange juice into a pitcher and put in the fridge to chill. Add the sparkling wine and stir gently just before the party. (About 8 servings.)

TWIST: YOU CAN SWAP THE TRIPLE SEC FOR GRAND MARNIER TO MAKE A GRAND MIMOSA.

'Champagne is just sparkling wine that knows someone.'

– Anonymous

Go Troppo

Nothing says 'vacay' like a tropical tipple. The best way to create a holiday vibe for an island-inspired happy hour is to get all your guests to come as tacky tourists. The guys can wear Hawaiian shirts and Bermuda shorts and the girls bright print dresses with big dabs of rouge. Fake tan is also de rigueur.

If not tourists, then ask your friends simply to dress as if they were going on a tropical holiday and wear sarongs or maxi-dresses. The men might sport anything from Panama hats and resortwear to nothing but a towel and a budgie carrier (men's swimming briefs). It's about whatever holidaywear means for them. If you serve a Hemingway daiquiri, you can also request the men emulate this icon of masculinity and don fake moustaches or grow real ones for the occasion. They could even wear safari suits.

A nice touch is to put garlands on your guests at the door. Or give the girls a flower for their hair, whether you pick blooms from the neighbour's garden or buy a bunch. Splurge on some tropical-looking colourful flowers to decorate your abode – even fake ones will do. Battery-operated candles, tea lights in shot glasses or tiny white lights are ideal for creating an outdoor ambience inside. Add some greenery and splashes of colour here and there. Perhaps cut some pineapples in half to stick cheese and other bite-sized snacks into. A vase full of oranges or any other fruit, even fake fruit, can help add to the festive atmosphere.

Ask your guests to send you their most embarrassing holiday snaps and print these out to use as laminated placemats and to plaster the walls. Funny holiday snaps make great icebreakers.

To help you get in the holiday mood, put your bikini on under your outfit, lather yourself with Hawaiian Tropic tanning oil and and watch Elvis in *Blue Hawaii* pre-party. You will almost be able to feel the sand in your toes.

Tropical Tipples

There is nothing like a taste of the tropics to get a soirée swinging. Even though these drinks remind us of summer, they are great for any season. Just like our sunny dispositions, they bring the weather with them. Add a slice of fruit for garnish or a little cocktail umbrella to each drink and hand them to guests along with a colourful napkin as they walk in the door.

I've provided recipes for single servings as well as quantities for a party-sized pitcher. I suggest serving these festive sips in cocktail glasses rather than tumblers. A cocktail glass adds a dash of glamour to any drink.

THE
Devilish
DAIQUIRI

**'THE TROUBLE WITH JOGGING IS THE
ICE FALLS OUT OF YOUR GLASS.'**

– Martin Mull

*This cocktail brings out everyone's naughty side. It's guaranteed to get the
festivities going. The daiquiri was first minted in Cuba and is one of its most
successful exports.*

Single serve

50ml white rum

25ml (1 tbsp + 2 tsp) lime juice

15ml (1 tbsp) simple syrup (see p.87)

ice cubes

Party pitcher

1x 750ml bottle white rum

375ml lime juice

225ml simple syrup (see p.87)

225ml chilled water

Single serve: Pour the rum, lime juice and simple syrup into a cocktail shaker
half filled with ice cubes. Shake well and strain into a chilled cocktail glass.

Pitcher: Combine all ingredients in a pitcher and stir well. Cover and keep in
the fridge. If possible, put the pitcher in the freezer for 2 to 3 hours before the
party so it's even more chilled. (About 15 servings.)

TWIST: YOU CAN SUBSTITUTE DARK RUM FOR WHITE, BUT THEN YOU SHOULD ALSO
CUT BACK A LITTLE ON THE SUGAR. YOU CAN ALSO USE LEMON JUICE IN PLACE OF
LIME IF YOU PREFER.

'ALWAYS DO SOBER WHAT YOU SAID YOU'D DO DRUNK. THAT WILL TEACH YOU TO KEEP YOUR MOUTH SHUT.'

– Ernest Hemingway

The late great writer Ernest Hemingway was a huge daiquiri fan and also a diabetic, so coined his own version with less sugar and more rum. I've halved the quantity of rum as he was an Olympian drinker. If you want a little history in a glass, then try this literary libation.

Single Serve

50ml white rum

25ml (1 tbsp + 2 tsp) lime juice

15ml (1 tbsp) maraschino liqueur

ice cubes

Party Pitcher

1 x 750ml bottle white rum

375ml lime juice

225ml maraschino liqueur

225ml chilled water

Single serve: Pour the rum, lime juice and maraschino liqueur into a cocktail shaker half filled with ice cubes. Shake well and strain into a chilled cocktail glass. Garnish with a maraschino cherry or a lime slice.

Pitcher: Combine all ingredients in a pitcher and stir well. Cover and keep in the fridge. If possible, put the pitcher in the freezer for 2 to 3 hours before the party so it's even more chilled. (About 15 servings.)

Party-Hard

**'IT TAKES ONLY ONE DRINK TO GET ME DRUNK.
THE TROUBLE IS, I CAN'T REMEMBER IF IT'S THE
THIRTEENTH OR THE FOURTEENTH.'**

– George Burns

Nothing says party like a piña colada. This paradisiacal potion has inspired its own song, countless romances and is the official beverage of Puerto Rico. It was created in the fifties by barman extraordinaire Ramon Marrero at the Caribe Hilton as a signature drink with star quality to satisfy its famous clientele.

Single Serve

50ml white rum

25ml (1 tbsp + 2 tsp) cream
   of coconut

50ml pineapple juice

ice cubes

Party Pitcher

1 x 750ml bottle of white rum

375ml cream of coconut

750ml pineapple juice

Single serve: Pour the rum, cream of coconut and pineapple juice into a cocktail shaker half filled with ice cubes. Shake well and strain into a chilled cocktail glass. Garnish with a maraschino cherry.

Pitcher: Combine all ingredients in a pitcher and stir well. Cover and keep in the fridge. If possible, put the pitcher in the freezer for 2 to 3 hours before the party so it's even more chilled. (About 15 servings.)

MARGARITA
Mayhem

'ONE TEQUILA, TWO TEQUILA, THREE TEQUILA, FLOOR.'

— George Carlin

The Margarita is one of the most popular of all party drinks. It's a disco in a glass. There are many myths about this mystical mix's creation but the most common one is that it was first made by a Mexican bartender in 1941 for a dazzling diva called Margarita Henkel, a siren who launched a thousand sips.

Single Serve

50ml tequila

25ml (1 tbsp + 2 tsp) triple sec

15ml (1 tbsp) lime juice

ice cubes

Party Pitcher

1 x 750ml bottle tequila

375ml triple sec

225ml lime juice

225ml chilled water

Single serve: Shake all ingredients in a cocktail shaker half filled with ice. Strain and serve in a cocktail or Margarita glass. If you like, dip the rim of the glass in lime juice and salt before pouring.

Pitcher: Combine all ingredients in a pitcher and stir well. Cover and keep in the fridge. If possible, put the pitcher in the freezer for 2 to 3 hours before the party so it's even more chilled. (About 15 servings.)

IF YOU LIKE IT HOTTER THAN MARCH IN THE MALDIVES, YOU CAN MAKE A JALAPEÑO MARGARITA. INFUSE A BOTTLE OF TEQUILA WITH TWO DE-SEEDED, DE-STEMMED, JULIENNED JALAPEÑO PEPPERS. KEEP IN THE FRIDGE FOR 1 TO 2 DAYS. USE THIS TEQUILA TO MAKE YOUR MARGARITA AND WATCH THE MERCURY RISE.

TEQUILA
Sunrise

'TAKE LIFE WITH A GRAIN OF SALT, A SLICE OF LIME AND A SHOT OF TEQUILA.'

– Anonymous

Single Serve

35ml (2 tbsp) tequila

50ml orange juice

15ml (1 tbsp) grenadine

ice cubes

Party Pitcher

1 x 750ml bottle tequila

1.2 litres orange juice

300ml grenadine

Single serve: If you want the full effect of the Tequila Sunrise, you will have to serve this in a tumbler. Put the grenadine in first. Then add ice, tequila and then orange juice and you will have a little sun in the bottom of the glass. I prefer to serve it in a cocktail glass and shake the ingredients over ice. Who needs to be reminded that it will be daylight tomorrow?

Pitcher: Combine all ingredients in a pitcher and stir well. Cover and keep in the fridge. If possible, put in the freezer for 2 to 3 hours before the party so it's even more chilled. (About 20 servings.)

'YOU'RE NOT DRUNK IF YOU CAN LIE ON THE FLOOR WITHOUT HOLDING ON.'

– Dean Martin

My friend Brendan Cullen invented this sublime drink. It's my new cocktail crush and will definitely get you in the tropical mood. It's like sipping sex through a straw.

Single Serve	*Party Pitcher*
50ml vanilla vodka	1 x 750ml bottle vanilla vodka
25ml (1 tbsp + 2 tsp) pineapple juice	375ml pineapple juice
7.5ml (1½ tsp) Rose's sweetened lime juice	115ml Rose's sweetened lime juice
7.5ml (1½ tsp) simple syrup (see p.87)	115ml simple syrup (see p.87)
	45ml chilled water

Single serve: Shake ingredients in a cocktail shaker half filled with ice. Strain and serve into a cocktail glass.

Pitcher: Combine ingredients in a pitcher and stir well. Cover and keep in the fridge. If possible, put the pitcher in the freezer for 2 to 3 hours before the party so it's even more chilled. (About 15 servings.)

Vegas Nights

These cocktail classics evoke the glamour of long hot nights at the casino, dressed to the nines as your life hangs on the spin of a roulette wheel. They bring to mind bad boys and every other temptation we know is not good for us but can't resist. For a Vegas Nights party, encourage your guests to dress as if they were a high roller going to the casino. Think faux diamond pinky rings and over the top glitz.

The look is flashy and trashy. If you need inspiration look to Sharon Stone in the movie *Casino* or Michelle Pfeiffer in *Scarface*. To look the part, don a sexy dress with a slit so high it can double as a gynaecological gown. Or you could even go as a Vegas showgirl. For this look, you can dress up a plain leotard or bathing suit with glue-on sequins and rhinestones. Add feathers to a tiara to wear as your headdress and don a pair of sexy fishnets and towering heels.

Whatever your outfit, make sure you accessorize with so much jewellery you flash like a Christmas tree. Feather boas are also a fun and flirty addition. Big hair, long painted nails and mad bling complete your look as an international woman of mystery. The guys can either try their best to look like a Mafia don or the dapper dudes in *Ocean's Eleven*. They can look to James Bond for inspiration or even the King of Vegas, Elvis. Even better if they can play the guitar and serenade you.

To decorate your apartment, perhaps get a friend who is good at Photoshop to morph a photo of you or one of your friends on to a dollar bill. You can blow these up and print them out to put on the walls and use as placemats. Alternatively, you could enlarge images of the Queen of Hearts or some of your guests' more outrageous casino snaps.

Casino stories are great conversational fodder. One way to get your guests talking is to ask them in advance for their best uncensored casino story. Type these up, make copies for every guest and give a prize to the person who matches the story to the right guest. This will give everybody a reason to mingle as well as adding grist to your story mill.

It's also fun to play roulette or any other Vegas-style games with Monopoly money. If you have a friend who loves card games, you can set him or her up as a croupier. If you want to up the ante, you can create bets that don't involve money but dares. It's all about living dangerously.

Lady Luck Libations

These classic drinks all make a perfect accessory for a hot Vegas night. They will make you throw caution to the wind and take a risk, whether it be on a game or on a handsome stranger. Be warned: they are so machismo they practically come with gold chains and chest hairs. Swarthy and full-bodied, drinking them is like putting a straw in Sean Connery.

THE
Sidecar

'HEALTH – WHAT MY FRIENDS ARE ALWAYS DRINKING TO BEFORE THEY FALL DOWN.'

– Phyllis Diller

The Sidecar is a classic vintage cocktail. It's quite a stiff pour and will get the party racing quicker than a Harley-Davidson. Harry's Bar in Paris is generally credited with concocting the Sidecar for a patron who, probably for the reasons above, rode in a sidecar.

Single Serve
50ml brandy

25ml triple sec

15ml (1 tbsp) lemon juice

ice cubes

Party Pitcher
1 x 750ml bottle brandy

375ml triple sec

225ml lemon juice

225ml water

Single serve: Shake ingredients in a cocktail shaker half filled with ice. Strain and serve in a cocktail glass. Garnish with an orange or lemon slice.

Pitcher: Combine all ingredients in a pitcher and stir well. Cover and keep in the fridge. If possible, put the pitcher in the freezer for 2 to 3 hours before the party so it's even more chilled. (About 15 servings.)

TWIST: USE BOURBON INSTEAD OF BRANDY TO MAKE A BOURBON SIDECAR. OR, IF YOU WANT TO SWEETEN IT UP, TRY SUBSTITUTING SPANISH BRANDY.

MAFIA'S

Kiss

'I SPENT A LOT OF MY MONEY ON BOOZE, BIRDS AND FAST CARS – THE REST I JUST SQUANDERED.'

– George Best

The perfect drink for a night of high rolling. Wear your sunglasses and cultivate a mysterious air as you sip. Don't imbibe it with anyone who looks like Don Corleone and carries a tyre iron.

Single Serve

50ml cranberry juice

35ml vodka

15ml (1 tbsp) amaretto

ice cubes

Party Pitcher

750ml cranberry juice

525ml vodka

225ml amaretto

225ml chilled water

Single serve: Shake ingredients in a cocktail shaker half filled with ice. Strain and serve in a cocktail glass.

Pitcher: Combine all ingredients in a pitcher and stir well. Cover and keep in the fridge. If possible, put the pitcher in the freezer for 2 to 3 hours before the party so it's even more chilled. (About 15 servings.)

CHANGE: ADD ¼ TEASPOON LIME JUICE FOR A BIT OF ADDED ZING TO THE SINGLE SERVING AND 112.5ML FOR THE PITCHER RECIPE.

'I DIDN'T FALL. THE FLOOR JUST NEEDED A HUG.'

– Anonymous

This oh-so-simple cocktail is one of my favourites. This medicinal beverage was invented by a naval surgeon to help prevent scurvy as the lime juice contains plenty of vitamin C. Believe me – it's just what the doctor ordered. Probably one of my favourite cocktails, but then I am a Lime Ho.

Single Serve

50ml gin or vodka

15ml (1 tbsp) Rose's sweetened
   lime juice

ice cubes

Party Pitcher

1 x 750ml bottle gin or vodka

225ml Rose's sweetened lime juice

225ml chilled water

Single serve: Shake ingredients in a cocktail shaker half filled with ice. Strain and serve in a cocktail glass. Garnish with a lime slice.

Pitcher: Combine all ingredients in a pitcher and stir well. Cover and keep in the fridge. If possible, put the pitcher in the freezer for 2 to 3 hours before the party so it's even more chilled. (About 15 servings.)

TWIST: ADD A DASH OF A FRUIT-BASED LIQUEUR FOR A SWEETER VARIATION. OR, USE A FRUIT-FLAVOURED VODKA, LIKE RASPBERRY OR PASSION FRUIT, INSTEAD OF PLAIN VODKA.

CLASSIC
Manhattan

'BETWEEN TWO EVILS I ALWAYS PICK THE ONE I NEVER TRIED BEFORE.'

– Mae West

The classic Manhattan has been around since the dawn of the cocktail era. It's simple, yet oh so sophistricated.

Single Serve
75ml bourbon

15ml (1 tbsp) sweet vermouth

ice cubes

Party Pitcher
1x 750ml bottle bourbon

150ml sweet vermouth

150ml water

Single serve: Half fill a shaker with ice cubes. Add the bourbon and vermouth and gently stir for 8 to 10 seconds, being careful not to break the ice cubes. Strain into a cocktail glass. Garnish with a maraschino cherry.

Pitcher: Combine all ingredients in a pitcher and stir well. Cover and keep in the fridge. If possible, put the pitcher in the freezer for 2 to 3 hours before the party so it's even more chilled. (About 10 servings.)

To get you in the mood to gamble on lady luck, watch one or all of these great gambling flicks: *Casino Royale, Croupier, The Cooler, Ocean's Eleven* and, of course, *Casino.*

Essential Bar Items

Make sure you have wine glasses and cocktail glasses or flutes if you are serving a bubbly cocktail. If you are serving Margaritas for your signature drink, you can serve these in Margarita glasses or cocktail glasses. It's also worthwhile having tumblers on hand for mixers. There is a high casualty rate for cocktail-party glassware, so make sure you have some plastic cups on hand. You will also need a plentiful supply of cocktail napkins. Hand these out with the first drink and keep some stashed at your improvised bar.

Forget jiggers and pourers. In order to work out quantities all you will need is a measuring jug with metric measurements and a tablespoon, which is equal to 15ml. Make sure you have whatever equipment you need to make your signature potion, whether this is a blender or cocktail stirrer (or long-handled spoon) and make sure you have a few pitchers for party-sized pours. A cocktail strainer is also useful, but any strainer that has small enough openings to catch ice cubes will do. You will need an ice bucket and ice tongs to add ice to drinks and a couple of bottle openers. Swizzle sticks or straws for guests to stir and sip from tumblers are also worthwhile.

The only other things you will need is a towel for spills and a bin for debris. And, lastly, a sense of humour.

Sizzling Soundtracks: We've put together playlists for all of these cocktail-party themes, whether Bubbly, Going Troppo or Hot Vegas Nights. There is also a 'Dance Your Ass Off' Party Mix for later in the night when your guests are in the mood to groove. GO TO MY WEBSITE AT BABESCOTT.COM TO LISTEN.

Martini Madness

Every hostess worthy of her cocktail shaker should learn how to make a martini. It's the ultimate in party chic.

> **The martini can transform any soirée into a swanky affair. IT'S THE ULTIMATE CHIC.**

*I*f you master only one cocktail, it should be the martini. It's a legend in a glass, and every hostess worthy of her shaker should know how to make one. The martini is to Cocktail Hour what the Chrysler building is to Manhattan: a timeless classic.

Probably the most famous cocktail in history, the martini is emblematic of Hollywood's Golden Era and has more screen credits than Meryl Streep. It has appeared alongside Marilyn Monroe and Bette Davis, to name a couple, and even inspired the famous line Robert Benchley uttered to Ginger Rogers in the classic film *The Major and the Minor*: 'Why don't you get out of that wet coat and into a dry martini?' Numerous politicians have fallen under its potent spell, from Winston Churchill to Franklin Roosevelt, who, not surprisingly, was in office when Prohibition was repealed. This captivating concoction has also fired the imagination of writers and scholars, from Hemingway to H. L. Mencken, who described it as 'the only American invention as perfect as a sonnet'. And, of course, the world's most famous fictional spy, James Bond, liked his Vesper martini 'shaken, not stirred'.

The sultan of suave, George Clooney, even claimed that he 'bought a nice piano once because I had the dream of playing "As Time Goes By" as some girl's leaning on it drinking a martini'. Poor fellow forgot he couldn't even play 'Chopsticks'. But that is what the martini does. This liquid legend overrides our rational brains and lets our romantic impulses take over. I would go so far as to say the martini has magical properties. This divine drink can transform even the shabbiest soirée into a swanky affair.

'He knows just how I like my martini. Full of alcohol.' – Homer Simpson ♥

The martini is all about old Hollywood, so I suggest you encourage your girlfriends to dress as bombshells and the men to dress in black tie. The martini isn't just a cocktail. It's an occasion. Don't insult this dazzling drink by dressing down. Find a painted-on dress that brings to mind the curves of Jayne Mansfield or Marilyn Monroe and makes you feel like a siren. And don't forget a pair of heels. You can't drink a martini in flat shoes – it doesn't taste the same. It's also imperative that you serve your martinis in martini glasses, even plastic ones. No other glass will do for the most sublime drink in the world.

Martini 101

The classic martini is made with dry vermouth and gin, with either an olive or a lemon twist for garnish. However, there are now so many variations on the original formula, it can make your head spin (especially if you sample all of them). Many modern versions substitute vodka for gin for a vodkatini. And there are any number of cocktails that don't include either vodka or gin but go by the name because they are served in a martini glass.

I prefer the gin martini. It's been described as 'liquid satin, fire and ice' by an anonymous aficionado and that pretty much sums it up. Many vixens, however, are as attached to their vodkatinis as Paris Hilton is to her Chihuahuas. Bond's Vesper martinis were made with vodka *and* gin. Beyond the gin or vodka debate, there is the issue of whether to shake or stir. The novelist Somerset Maugham professed that 'martinis should always be stirred, not shaken, so that the molecules lie sensuously one on top of the other'.

I recommend stirring if you're turning out volume for a party. Otherwise, you may have to shake so many martinis you end up with carpal tunnel syndrome. You don't have to serve both vodka and gin martinis; simply serve your preferred potion. After all, you're not trying to compete with a cocktail bar. Rather, you're trying to introduce the palates of your heathen friends to your recipe for martini heaven. Below are the steps to devising the perfect martini for your party.

1. CHOOSE YOUR POTION

If you haven't tried a martini before, this is one drink that should go on the ice-bucket list. Head down to a local bar with a friend and try both a vodka and a gin martini to see which spirit base you prefer. Suit your own preferences and budget when it comes to brands. Gordon's is a quality gin that won't put your wallet in traction. It was also the preferred gin of James Bond. (In *Casino Royale*, Bond specified Gordon's for his Vesper martini.) If it's good enough for a super-spy, it's certainly good enough for me. And there are plenty of cheap vodkas, from Smirnoff to Chekov. There are also flavoured vodkas you can sample to give your martini a twist.

2. HOW MANY TO HORIZONTAL?

I wouldn't serve guests more than two or three martinis because your party may just go from madness to mayhem. Dorothy Parker once infamously said: 'I like to have a martini, two at the very most. After three I'm under the table, after four I'm under my host.' Take the writer's words as a cautionary tale. The stuff is rocket fuel, so beware and encourage your guests to sip rather than guzzle. Martinis really bring out the devil in a person. After one or two, encourage your guests to switch to beer, wine or soft drinks. Or keep drinking at your own risk – but don't say I didn't warn you.

3. THE VERMOUTH DILEMMA

While the classic martini recipe calls for 15ml of vermouth, feel free to alter it to taste. The more gin or vodka relative to the amount of vermouth, the drier the martini. Many die-hard martini drinkers like their martinis drier than Mae West's wit. Clark Gable in the movie *Teacher's Pet* just moistened the cork of the vermouth bottle and dabbed it in his martini to get the right ratio. And Noel Coward recommended the perfect martini be made by 'filling a glass with gin and then waving it in the general direction of Italy' (to get a whiff of vermouth). And one committed martini drinker told me he just opens the bottle of vermouth and puts a fan near it so some of the molecules seep into his martini.

4. ICE QUEEN COLD

The martini should be served colder than a mother-in-law's kiss. That is, at a positively arctic temperature. Keep your martini pitcher in the refrigerator and put it in the freezer for 2 to 3 hours before the party to make it even colder. If you have room, you can chill your glasses in the freezer for a couple of hours or in the fridge for 3 to 4 hours. Alternatively, you can fill a bowl with ice, swirl it around and throw it out before pouring the martini. After the first round, leave the pitchers in ice buckets at your bar station for guests to serve themselves.

5. DON'T FORGET THE GARNISH

I don't care about other drinks, but I think a martini without an olive is like Bonnie without Clyde. They are partners in crime. Traditionally, you use one or three olives on a toothpick. Four is too many and two olives is a faux pas. It's urban folklore that two olives used to be a sign of danger for martini-loving Mafia. Apparently, if a barman served a martini with two olives it meant there was a threat in the room, be it another Mob boss or an undercover cop. So if your new gold-chain-wearing friend Luis and his gang hightail it home, you will know the double-trouble garnish was probably the cause.

Martinis really bring out the DEVIL in a person.

THE CLASSIC
Martini

It's worth trying this classic martini recipe with both vodka and gin. If you want to experiment further you can test-drive the vermouth ratios. Once you find the perfect martini then life will be complete!

Single Serve

75ml of vodka or gin

15ml (1 tbsp) vermouth

ice cubes

Party Pitcher

1 x 750ml bottle vodka or gin

150ml vermouth

150ml chilled water

Single serve: Pour the vodka or gin and vermouth into a cocktail shaker half filled with ice cubes. Shake well and strain into a chilled cocktail glass. Garnish with an olive.

Pitcher: Combine all ingredients in a pitcher and stir gently. Keep refrigerated and put in the freezer for 2 to 3 hours before your guests arrive so it's nice and cold. (Makes 13½ servings.)

JAMES BOND MARTINI: The 007 martini has both gin and vodka. This Molotov cocktail in a glass was made famous in *Casino Royale* and was named after the suave spy's love interest, sexy agent Vesper Lynd. She asked if he named it after her because of its 'bitter aftertaste'. In true swashbuckling style, Bond replied that he named it after her 'because once you've tasted it, you won't drink anything else'. This unforgettable drink is made with 90ml gin, 30ml vodka and 15ml (1 tbsp) Lillet Blanc wine. Bond famously likes his martinis shaken not stirred, so shake this sublime drink in a shaker half filled with ice and strain into a cocktail glass or a champagne goblet.

The beertini is where glamour meets ESPN. It's footballer meets femme fatale. This cocktail is a little five o'clock stubble in a martini glass – a splash of liquid testosterone with a little touch of class. It proves beer can be chic and peach vodka can behave without a shred of decorum.

Single Serve	*Party Pitcher*
35ml (2 tbsp) peach-flavoured vodka	420ml peach-flavoured vodka
15ml (1 tbsp) peach schnapps	180ml peach schnapps
15ml (1 tbsp) cranberry juice	180ml cranberry juice
70ml Stella Artois beer	3 x 284ml bottles Stella Artois beer

Single serve: Pour the peach vodka, schnapps, cranberry juice and beer into a shaker and stir. Pour into a chilled martini glass.

Pitcher: Pour vodka, schnapps and cranberry juice into a pitcher and keep refrigerated. Pour in the beer and stir just before the party so it doesn't go too flat. (About 10 servings.)

Martini Variations

There are plenty of simple variations on the martini if you want to add some flair. Here are some ideas for a martini with a twist:

Dirty Martini: Add a dash of olive brine to a classic gin martini. You can buy olive juice or simply reserve it from the olive jar. Add a couple of dashes if you like it filthy.

Pickle Martini: Substitute pickle juice for olive brine and add a gherkin as garnish if you like.

Bitter But Not Twisted: Add a dash of bitters to spice up either a classic gin or vodka martini.

Lychee Martini: Substitute lychee liqueur for vermouth in a vodka martini.

Apple Martini: 50ml vodka, 30ml green apple schnapps.

Tequini: Subsitute tequila for the vodka or gin and add a dash of bitters.

Smokey Martini: Substitute whisky for vermouth in a gin martini.

'A man must defend his home, his wife, his children, and his martini.'

– Jackie Gleason

'I had never tasted anything so cool and clean. They made me feel civilized.'

– Ernest Hemingway describing the martini in *A Farewell to Arms*

'If it wasn't for the olives in his martinis, he'd starve to death!'

– Milton Berle

'The martini is the supreme American gift to world culture.'

– Bernard DeVoto

It's easy as sin to create

tempting party fare.

The secrets to preparing
no-fuss, fiendishly delicious finger food.

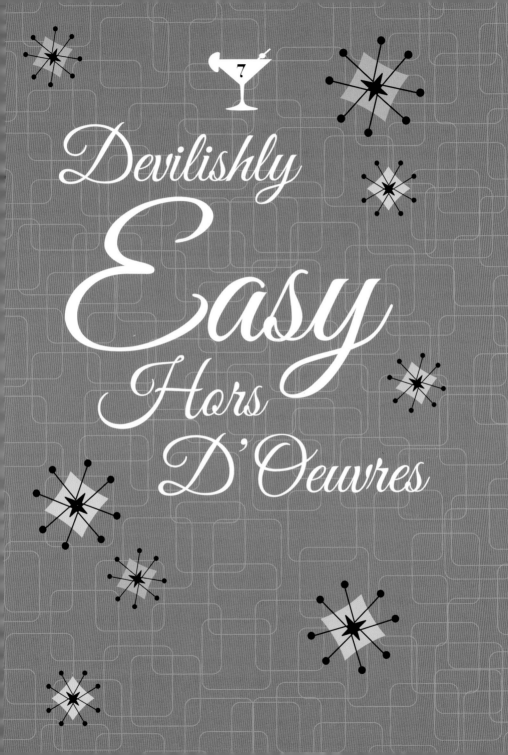

7

Devilishly Easy Hors D'Oeuvres

$\mathcal{I}$f you want your cocktail parties to have staying power, you will need to provide some sustenance. Olives on a toothpick don't constitute dinner even if you drink so many martinis that your favourite garnish would turn up in a urine test. And passing around the Kraft cheese slices isn't going to win you any social kudos (let alone snag you a stud). If you want to impress, you will need some fabulous finger food both to wow your guests' tastebuds and to soak up all that fine alcohol.

It's really not that hard to feed people, especially after they've had a drink or two. After the first cocktail, my friends are like a flock of seagulls who would fight over a crust or half a doughnut. A drink or a few make your guests very receptive to your culinary offerings. And cocktail food is the easiest. You can dress up nearly anything edible as an hors d'oeuvre, or, as I like to call them, 'whores d'oeuvres'. As long as your cocktail food is bite-sized and tasty, your guests will devour it. Trust me, they would probably eat a vat of Brigitte Nielsen's liposuction if it were rolled into faux cheese balls.

So don't stress. I'm going to help you get past your culinary phobia and stare down the few dishes that stand between you and your rightful role of cocktail-party queen. I'm going to demystify party food so you can see just how easy and fun creating a menu for mischief can be.

Basically, cocktail-party fare consists of small, savoury finger foods that can be eaten in one or two mouthfuls. Using the tips and recipes in this chapter, you can plan out your cocktail menu weeks in advance or even the day before . . . it's really that simple.

I've outlined the steps to a scrumptious soirée and included crowd-pleasing recipes that you can whip up without breaking into a sweat or risking a hangnail. All the ingredients can be found at your supermarket, if not your local deli and many of the staples I've suggested can be used in multiple recipes. And they are all budget friendly. I've ensured that you will have money and time to spare for a blow-dry and a trip to the nail salon.

Planning Your Menu

I've given you plenty of delicious recipes to choose from later in this chapter, but before getting out your mixing bowls, you'll need to do some figuring so you don't end up with too much food, too little food or spending way too much time in the kitchen when you should be schmoozing your guests and swilling cocktails.

As far as how much to allow, the rule of thumb is to provide five to six different hors d'oeuvres, figuring roughly two per person of each type if you are hosting a cocktail party outside mealtimes. If you are holding a soirée during dinner, or hosting a famished football team (in which case, invite me over), then seven to eight hors d'oeuvres are recommended. It's also worth having some snacks on hand for when the finger food runs out. I've outlined some snack ideas overleaf. And, if you bought the list of Sexy Staples on pages 34-5, you will already have them standing by.

Variety is the spice of life, so make sure there is a range of choices on your cocktail menu. Consider pesky vegetarians and include a couple of meatless options. But other than a token vegetable or two, don't worry about catering to any diet. Cocktail food is meant to be delicious and indulgent. By and large, many of the finger-food recipes in this chapter can be made the morning of the party, if not well in advance, so there is no last-minute scrambling. Remember, you're supposed to spend a good portion of your party day primping and

'Consider **PESKY VEGETARIANS** *and include a couple of meatless options.'* ❤

preening and otherwise upping your fabulousness quotient. The one exception to this is any dish that's meant to be served warm. Obviously, you'll have to do any heating-up just before your guests arrive, but you can still assemble most of these dishes the day before so they are oven-ready. Then all you have to do is take them out of the fridge and pop them in a pre-heated oven just before your guests arrive. To keep things simple, I would suggest serving only a few warm dishes that you bring out early to save you from running around with too many hot plates.

Enlist the help of friends to pass plates of food around as the party is getting started. This will save you the effort and give your friends (especially the shy ones) an excuse to mingle with other guests and gain instant popularity. Once each plate has done a few rounds, put it down on a makeshift buffet or any handy surface and let guests help themselves.

Luscious Leftovers

First things first: start with what you've got. Make sure to consult your pantry and fridge as you plan your menu. My mom always used to say 'Waste not, want not' and I'm of the same school of thought. Why let quality goods go to waste? I recycle everything: jokes, ex-boyfriends, clothing, gifts and certainly everything in my fridge and pantry. You'd be surprised what you can turn into a whores d'oeuvre. Cocktail parties present an opportunity to go through all the assorted produce, packaged products and odd bits of food that you have in your kitchen before they are past their use-by date. I've put together this entire section with leftovers (and laziness) in mind.

I've put all the cocktail foods in sections so you can see how easy it is to mix and match to create different types of hors d'oeuvres. Simply scan each section for ideas and compare it to what you have, then plan your menu from there.

If you scour the contents of your fridge and pantry you might well be able to create an instant cocktail menu supplemented by a few items bought from the corner shop. For instance, there are any number of foodstuffs you can pair with toasted baguette slices to create yummy crostinis. Chances are you will also have at least some of the ingredients to create if not 'Pigs in Pashminas' then another doughy delight.

If you have leftover soup or even canned soup, you can heat it up and serve it warm (not scalding) in shot glasses. If it's a chunky soup, put it in the blender until it's smooth so your guests don't encounter any choking hazards as they 'shoot their soup'. Just make sure whatever soup you serve is seasoned well. You can add a dab of sour cream to roasted red pepper, butternut squash, pumpkin or mushroom soup for extra zing.

Make sure you also put out whatever snacks you have to hand. They don't have to be fancy. I like the faithful old standbys that have been around since my grandmother was getting soused at her sneak-a-spot-of-sherry quilting club: pretzels, salty roasted peanuts, almonds or any mixed nuts. You can also offer bowls of plain potato crisps, Ritz crackers, Twiglets, breadsticks, olives or any other goodies you have on hand. In a fit of desperation, I've even been known to put out bowls of Froot Loops.

Delicious Dips

You can also create delicious dips from leftover packet soup. Just add a tub of sour cream to almost any packet soup: for instance, onion, mushroom, vegetable or tomato. Simply blend the sour cream and soup mixture together in a food processor and add salt and pepper to taste. If you are running short of sour cream, you can substitute yoghurt, cream cheese or even mayonnaise for up to a third of the sour cream.

Serve these dips with leftover vegetables cut into crudités, which is a fancy term for veggies cut into strips and served with dip. You can use baby sticks of carrot, celery, cucumber, peppers, broccoli or cauliflower florets, and even spears of romaine lettuce. There are also plenty of pre-made dips you can buy if you are pressed for time. Among my own personal faves are hummus, taramasalata and aubergine, but you can't go wrong with any flavour that takes your fancy.

Just use your imagination and you won't have to stretch your wallet or walk too far to create a mouthwatering menu.

'Too much of a good thing can be WONDERFUL.'

– Mae West

If you have any leftover main dishes like macaroni cheese or meatloaf, you can turn these into mini savoury cupcakes. Seriously, almost anything can be turned into Last Night's Dinner Cupcakes. Simply throw the dinner into your food processor and pulse till it's all blended. Then throw in some salt and pepper to taste. Thaw a couple of sheets of frozen puff pastry and cut into 24 rounds with a 6cm-diameter tumbler. Then spray a non-stick 24-cup mini-muffin tin with cooking spray and put the dough rounds into the muffin cups, moulding them to fit and making sure they come right up the sides. (It's really worthwhile investing in a non-stick muffin tin. The regular ones are a bugger to clean.) Scoop a teaspoon or so of the mixture into the muffin cups to fill them. Sprinkle some grated cheese on top and then bake these little cupcake cuties for 15 to 18 minutes at 180°C. And *voilà*: you have 24 adorable mini cupcakes that your friends will be oohing and aahing over reincarnated from the boring old bolognese you scoffed last night.

Savoury mini-cupcakes are a great way

to re-purpose comfort food.

Popcorn is like that little black shirt you can wear a million ways. It's a snack that's easy to dress up or down and is consistently YUMMY.

While plain old popcorn works a treat, you can add almost anything to it to give it a bit of zing. Just have a look at whatever herbs, spices and seasonings you have skulking around in your pantry and sprinkle them on to your popcorn after you've added some melted butter to help them stick. The following are a few simple ways to give your popcorn some pizzazz.

First, you will need salted, butter-free, microwavable popcorn. Pop 225g of kernels for each recipe (which will make a party-sized bowl of popped popcorn). Then melt 60g of butter to coat it before adding the flavouring. As an option, you can also add 60ml of olive oil to lightly coat. Throw it all in a large bowl while warm and mix. You can also add some finely chopped chives or parsley to give some colour.

Parmesan Popcorn

40g grated Parmesan cheese.

Toss with buttered popcorn.

Paprika Popcorn

1 tsp salt, ½ tsp smoked paprika.

Toss with buttered popcorn.

Mexican Style

1 tbsp fajita seasoning.

Toss with buttered popcorn.

Curry Popcorn

1 tsp curry powder.

Toss with buttered popcorn.

The Four Main Cocktail Food Groups

The four food groups – Cheesy, Doughy, Meaty and Bacony – form the fundamentals of fabulous cocktail food. Cocktail parties thrive on decadence and these flirty food-stuffs are so fiendishly delicious they are positively sinful. And sin tastes good, real good. As Homer Simpson said: 'You don't win friends with salad.' Cocktail food is about coronary-inducing, caution-to-the-wind naughtiness. It's about leaving our diets and sense of decorum behind and indulging our hedonistic sides.

'You don't win friends with **SALAD'**♥

Cocktails and Cheesy snacks are the perfect pairing, like Beyoncé and Jay-Z. They go together like candyfloss and amusement parks, beer and the Super Bowl, vodka and rappers. Doughy delights are also the stuff of great soirées. They are ideal for feeding and filling up the hungry hordes. That's why my cocktail parties feature more carbs than a pre-marathon buffet.

A cocktail party also has to include some meaty morsels. There's nothing like a couple of cocktails to make you crave something carnivorous. And no party is complete without a bacony bite or two. Bacon is the bad boy of the culinary world – naughty but irresistible. The stuff is so darn tempting it could have been created by the devil himself. Hosting a party without bacony hors d'oeuvres is like holding the Golden Globes without asking Ricky Gervais.

Throw your diet to the winds and think indulgence when planning your cocktail menu.

Cheesy

Cheese goes with everything, particularly alcohol. It's versatile, yummy and easy to use. It's the ideal go-to staple for every Lazy Hostess. Put out a cheese plate and you will be everybody's instant best friend. There are plenty of other ways you can use cheese to make delicious hors d'oeuvres. It's an ideal ingredient for a crostini. It's delicious in a pastry blanket and captivating on a kebab. You can even just cut it up into cubes and put it on a tray to eat with toothpicks, by itself or paired with pieces of pineapple, gherkins or olives. You can never overdo the cheese at a cocktail party. Here are some more cheesy ideas.

GARNISHES: You don't need to worry too much about garnishes. Take a cue from Chinese restaurants and just throw a sprig of parsley on everything. Or you can use tiny slivers of chive to add a touch of green, or other leftover herbs if you feel so inclined. I've suggested specific garnishes for a few of the hors d'oeuvre recipes but only where these garnishes add flavour. And if you run out of parsley or just can't be bothered, the best garnish for any dish is simply your hundred-watt smile.

BRIE'S NOT A
Bitch

SERVE WARM
SERVES 12

It might seem posh, but baked Brie is a very approachable dish. It's super-simple to make and, trust me, if you serve this your guests will think you are 'brie-lliant'.

1 sheet ready-rolled frozen puff pastry, thawed

plain flour for dusting

3–4 tbsp strawberry or apricot jam

20g sliced almonds, or chopped walnuts

250g Brie

1 egg

1. Preheat oven to 180°C. Line a rimmed baking sheet with parchment paper.
2. Lightly flour your surface and roll out the pastry sheet. Trim the corners to the shape of the cheese. Spread jam evenly over the sheet to within 5cm of the edges. Sprinkle nuts on top.
3. Place the Brie in the centre of the pastry. Fold the pastry over the cheese to cover and seal the edges with your fingers. Place the cheese seam side down on the parchment-lined baking sheet.
4. Beat the egg in a small bowl. Brush the pastry with egg and bake for 25 minutes or until golden brown. Remove from oven and let stand for 15 minutes. Accompany with crackers.
* Brushing the pastry with egg is a must or it won't become golden brown.

YOU CAN PREPARE THIS A DAY IN ADVANCE AND KEEP IT IN THE FRIDGE COVERED IN CLING FILM. BAKE JUST BEFORE YOUR GUESTS ARRIVE.

POTATO-CRISP CRUSTED
Cheese Balls

MAKES 24

Potato crisps and cheese are an inspired combination. Try these balls of flavour and you will be instantly addicted.

500g cream cheese, softened

1 level tbsp onion soup mix

125g Cheddar cheese, grated

1 x 25g packet low-salt potato crisps

1. Combine cream cheese, soup mix and Cheddar cheese in a mixing bowl.
2. Shape mixture into small balls and place on a lined baking sheet.
3. Put the crisps in a food processor and pulse until they are crumbed. Roll the balls in the crumbs until coated.
4. Cover the baking sheet with cling film and chill the cheese balls for at least an hour and up to a day in the fridge so they become firm.

THESE CAN BE MADE A DAY IN ADVANCE AND KEPT COVERED IN THE FRIDGE. IF YOU ARE MAKING THEM IN A HURRY, YOU CAN MAKE THE BALLS AND PUT THEM IN THE FREEZER TO CHILL FOR 10 MINUTES BEFORE SERVING.

CHEF'S SECRET BAKING TIP: My friend, sexy chef Dave Hart, gave me this tip, which will ensure that none of your baked dishes burn on the backside like an English tourist on the beach. Simply double up on your baking sheets if you are baking only one dish in a conventional oven, or put an empty baking dish on the rack below. This is because in a conventional oven the heat comes from the bottom and moves upwards. You can ignore this tip if you are one of those lucky souls who has a fan assisted oven, which moves heat evenly.

Lazy Nut
CHEESE LOG

SERVES 12

Cheese, peanuts and bacon are the unholy trinity when it comes to wickedly good hors d'oeuvres. This nut cheese log is so tasty it will make your toes curl.

60g roasted, salted peanuts

2 rashers streaky bacon, cooked and chopped

250g cream cheese, softened

40g grated Parmesan cheese

1. Put the peanuts in a food processor and pulse until crumbed. Remove half the crumbed nuts and set aside. Add bacon and pulse until finely chopped. Then add cream cheese and Parmesan and pulse till blended.
2. Put the mixture on to parchment paper and use your hands to shape into a 20cm log. Place the remaining crumbed nuts on a fresh sheet of parchment and roll the log in the nuts until coated.
3. Wrap in cling film and refrigerate for at least 2 hours and up to 2 days until it becomes firm. Serve with crackers.
* You can swap the salted peanuts for pretzels if you like.

THIS CAN BE MADE A DAY OR TWO IN ADVANCE AND KEPT IN THE FRIDGE COVERED IN CLING FILM.

> '*Alcohol may be man's worst enemy*
>
> *but the Bible says love your enemy.*'
>
> – Frank Sinatra

Party
PUFFS

Another great hors d'oeuvre that has stood the test of time is the cheese puff. It's as classic and elegant as Grace Kelly.

120ml water	4 large eggs, at room temperature
120ml milk	150g Cheddar cheese, grated
110g butter	twist of ground pepper
½ tsp salt	pinch of nutmeg
125g plain flour	

1. Preheat oven to 200°C. Line a rimmed baking sheet with parchment paper.
2. In a medium saucepan, combine water, milk, butter and salt and bring to the boil.
3. Add flour and stir with a spoon until a smooth dough forms. Continue stirring over low heat until the dough dries out and pulls away from the pan: about 2 minutes.
4. Scrape the dough into a bowl. Let cool for 1 minute and add eggs one at a time, stirring thoroughly after each one. Add cheese and a pinch of pepper and nutmeg.
5. Transfer dough into a freezer bag with the corner cut off and pipe tablespoon-sized mounds, about 3cm wide by 2cm long on to the baking sheet, 5cm apart. With a wet finger, lightly press down the swirl at the top of each puff. Bake for about 20 minutes.
* You can use mature Cheddar if you like to add more zing. For even more flavour you can add 2 teaspoons of chopped fresh thyme.

YOU CAN COOK THE PUFFS WEEKS AHEAD AND FREEZE THEM IN A FREEZER BAG WITH THE AIR SQUEEZED OUT. DEFROST AT ROOM TEMPERATURE FOR AROUND 30 MINUTES AND REHEAT FOR 10 MINUTES IN THE OVEN AT 180°C.

Mozzarella
AND TOMATO BITES

MAKES 24

Mozzarella with cherry tomatoes and basil is deceptively simple and absolutely delicious.

120ml balsamic vinegar

60ml olive oil

½ tsp salt

¼ tsp ground pepper

24 mini mozzarella balls (about 450g)

24 cherry tomatoes

24 small basil leaves

toothpicks

1. Mix the balsamic vinegar, oil, salt and pepper together in a bowl.
2. Add the mozzarella to the balsamic mixture. Cover with cling film and let marinate in the fridge for at least 1 hour and up to 2 days.
3. Allow cheeses to return to room temperature before threading one each on a jumbo toothpick along with a cherry tomato and a small basil leaf on top.

THIS CAN BE MADE THE MORNING OF THE PARTY AND KEPT COVERED IN THE FRIDGE.

FETA AND
Watermelon
SPIKES

MAKES 24

Feta and watermelon are a tantalizing combination that proves opposites attract.

1 small watermelon wedge (about 450g), chilled

200g feta

24 small mint leaves

ground pepper

toothpicks

1. Remove rind and seeds from the watermelon and cut flesh into 24 bite-sized cubes.
2. Cut cheese into roughly 2.5cm squares.
3. Skewer 1 cheese cube and 1 square of watermelon on to each jumbo toothpick along with a small mint leaf. Sprinkle with black pepper and serve.
*Cantaloupe or honeydew are also flavoursome with feta if you want to substitute these.

THESE NEED TO BE MADE RIGHT BEFORE THE PARTY STARTS OR THE WATERMELON MAY GO SOGGY.

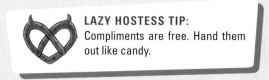

LAZY HOSTESS TIP:
Compliments are free. Hand them out like candy.

Sexy
CHEESE SPEARS

MAKES 24

Endive leaves are naughty but nice when teamed with decadent cheese and wanton walnuts.

150g Boursin cheese

2 large heads Belgian endive, trimmed and separated into leaves

24 walnut halves, toasted

1. Use a teaspoon to place a dollop of Boursin on the end of each endive spear. Top with a piece of toasted walnut. Serve cold.

*The mellow flavour of Boursin works well with the endive, but you can substitute any flavourful soft cheese or mild blue cheese. You could also top with crumbled bacon instead of walnuts.

THESE CAN BE MADE THE MORNING OF THE PARTY AND KEPT COVERED IN THE FRIDGE.

'I can resist anything but temptation.'

– Oscar Wilde

MAD FOR *Mozzarella* STICKS

Mozzarella sticks are as comforting and classic as a Billy Joel song. This pub staple is also perfect for cocktail parties and will make your barfly friends so happy they will want to sing like a piano man.

500g log fresh mozzarella

2 eggs

90g Italian-seasoned breadcrumbs

110g finely grated Parmesan

vegetable oil for frying

1. Cut mozzarella log lengthwise into sticks, about 2.5cm by 10cm.
2. In a medium bowl, beat eggs until well blended.
3. Mix breadcrumbs, Parmesan and salt in a bowl until blended.
4. Coat the cheese in the egg mixture, then dip into the breadcrumb mixture until completely coated. Shake off excess crumbs and dip in egg and then breadcrumb mixture a second time.
5. Place on a parchment-lined baking sheet or platter and put in the fridge to firm for a minimum of 1 hour and up to 2 days.
6. Heat oil in a frying pan over medium-high heat and fry the mozzarella sticks until golden brown: about 3 to 4 minutes each side.
7. Remove from the pan and place on kitchen paper to soak up the excess oil. Accompany with marinara sauce.
* If you can't find Italian seasoned breadcrumbs, simply mix 90g plain breadcrumbs with 1 tbsp Italian seasoning.

YOU CAN PREPARE THESE A DAY IN ADVANCE AND STORE THEM COVERED IN THE FRIDGE. COOK THEM THE MORNING OF THE PARTY AND HEAT THEM IN THE MICROWAVE BEFORE THE GUESTS ARRIVE.

DARING

Dates

MAKES 24

Dates and goat's cheese are a match made in culinary heaven.

200g fresh goat's cheese, softened

24 dates, halved and stoned

24 roasted pecans

1. Spoon a heaped teaspoon of goat's cheese into each of the halved dates. Or, even easier, pipe it through a slit in the cheese packet or cut the corner from a sandwich bag and pipe through the slit.

2. Add a pecan to the top of each. Serve immediately or refrigerate, covered, for up to 4 hours. Bring back to room temperature before serving.

* If you don't have pecans, you can use walnuts or almonds. You can also use cream cheese if you like.

THESE CAN BE MADE THE MORNING OF THE PARTY AND KEPT COVERED IN THE FRIDGE.

LAZY HOSTESS TIP: If you suffer from name amnesia like me, just call everyone 'Sweetie' and 'Dahling'.

AMOROUS

Apricots

MAKES 24

These are so simple yet positively scrumptious. They are a must on any Lazy Hostess's cocktail menu.

110g Stilton

splash of milk

ground black pepper

24 dried apricots

85g honey

24 roasted and salted pistachios

1. Mix Stilton in a blender with a touch of milk and a pinch of black pepper until smooth. Using a teaspoon, dollop a bit of the cheese mixture on each apricot. Or, even easier, cut the corner from a sandwich bag and pipe a small amount through the slit on to each apricot.

2. Drizzle with a small amount of honey and top with a pistachio nut.

3. Arrange apricots on a platter and serve.

THESE CAN BE MADE THE MORNING OF THE PARTY AND KEPT COVERED IN THE FRIDGE.

Doughy

$\mathcal{C}$ ocktail parties are social marathons in heels. This is why carbohydrates are essential. A steady supply of carbs will help your guests maintain their stamina for imbibing and socializing. They will give your cocktail parties staying power. This is why you should feature at least a couple of items from the *Doughy* food family.

CROWD-PLEASING CROSTINIS

Crowd-pleasing Crostinis: Some of the easiest doughy hors d'oeuvres to make are crostinis. *Crostini* is an Italian word meaning 'little toasts'. It's basically a fancy term for baguette slices that have been brushed with olive oil and baked until golden. You then put toppings on them to create fabulous party fare. It's a cinch to create any number of mouthwatering crostini combinations. You can mix and match many of the foodstuffs in your fridge or follow the foolproof recipes in this section.

MAKES 24

Even someone with two arms in a sling could manage to assemble this simple yet scrumptious hors d'oeuvre.

1 long baguette

olive oil

250g cream cheese

24 sun-dried tomatoes (about 120g)

ground pepper

1. Preheat oven to 200°C. Cut baguette into ½ cm slices and arrange them on a baking sheet lined with parchment paper.

2. Brush the top of the crostinis with oil and bake for around 10 minutes until they are lightly toasted.

3. Spread the crostinis with cream cheese and sprinkle with diced sun-dried tomatoes. Season with pepper.

THESE CAN BE MADE THE MORNING OF THE PARTY AND KEPT COVERED IN THE FRIDGE.

I'M EASY CHEESE DIP: This cheese dip needs to be served warm but is scrumptious and simple to make. When you pass it around to eligible cuties emphasize the 'I'm Easy' part of the title with a knowing wink. Bring 250ml milk and 2 tablespoons plain flour to a simmer, whisking continuously to prevent it lumping. Add 250g grated Cheddar cheese and keep whisking until smooth. Add 1 tablespoon Dijon mustard and blend. Accompany with toasted baguette rounds. Nothing goes down quite so easily.

SERVE WARM

MAKES 24

Even if you have an uneasy relationship with crustaceans, you will love this crab crostini. It's where the sea meets sophistication.

1 long baguette

olive oil

170g canned crab meat

½ tsp East End Fish Seasoning

250g cream cheese

1. Preheat oven to 200°C. Cut baguette into ½ cm slices and arrange them on a baking sheet lined with parchment paper.
2. Brush the top of the crostinis with oil and bake for around 10 minutes until they are lightly toasted.
3. Drain the crab meat. Mix with East End Fish Seasoning and cream cheese.
4. Spread the mixture on the crostinis. Garnish with a sprig of parsley.

THESE CAN BE MADE THE MORNING OF THE PARTY AND KEPT COVERED IN THE FRIDGE.

SCENE-STEALING
Salmon

MAKES 24

Salmon and cream cheese are as indomitable a duo as Patsy and Edina. They also go just as well with wine.

1 long baguette

olive oil

250g cream cheese

100g smoked salmon

1 x 99g jar capers

1. Preheat oven to 200°C. Cut baguette into ½ cm slices and arrange them on a baking sheet lined with parchment paper.
2. Brush the top of the crostinis with oil and bake for around 10 minutes until they are lightly toasted.
3. Spread the crostinis with cream cheese and add a small slice of smoked salmon. Add a few capers for extra zing.
* Add a couple of slices of red onion if you like even more bite.

THESE CAN BE MADE THE MORNING OF THE PARTY AND KEPT COVERED IN THE FRIDGE.

ONION *Love*

MAKES 24

The humble onion transforms into a sultry tongue-tempter once it's caramelized. Add a little cream cheese and it's simply irresistible.

1 long baguette

olive oil

3 large onions, thinly sliced

½ tsp salt

1 tbsp brown sugar

1 tbsp balsamic vinegar

125g goat's cheese

1. Preheat oven to 200°C. Cut baguette into ½ cm slices and arrange them on a baking sheet lined with parchment paper.
2. Brush the top of the crostinis with oil and bake for around 10 minutes until they are lightly toasted.
3. Heat 2 tablespoons of oil in a frying pan over medium heat. Add onions, sprinkle with salt and sauté until softened, stirring frequently: about 5 minutes.
4. Add brown sugar and vinegar, and keep stirring occasionally until the onions are caramelized: another 15 to 20 minutes. If the onions dry out, add a splash of water, wine or stock.
5. Spread the crostinis with goat's cheese and add a teaspoon of the onion mixture on top.

THE CARAMELIZED ONIONS CAN BE MADE THE DAY BEFORE AND KEPT COVERED IN THE FRIDGE. THE CROSTINIS CAN BE ASSEMBLED THE MORNING OF THE PARTY. YOU WILL NEED TO HEAT THESE IN A PREHEATED OVEN AT 230°C FOR 1 MINUTE TO TAKE THE CHILL OFF.

 LAZY HOSTESS TIP: Put a piece of bread in your brown sugar to stop it going harder than Peter Andre's abs.

Magic MUSHROOMS

MAKES 24

These mushroom crostinis taste so magical they will have your guests hallucinating that they are in a fancy restaurant.

1 long baguette

olive oil

250g button mushrooms

½ tbsp salt

250g cream cheese (or goat's cheese), softened

ground pepper

1. Preheat oven to 200°C. Cut baguette into ½ cm slices and arrange them on a baking sheet lined with parchment paper.
2. Brush the top of the crostinis with oil and bake for around 10 minutes until they are lightly toasted.
3. Clean the mushrooms, trim and slice. Heat 2 tablespoons of oil in a frying pan over medium heat.
* Mushrooms absorb water, which is why it's better to clean them by rubbing with kitchen paper rather than washing them in water.
4. Put mushrooms in the frying pan in a single layer and sauté over medium heat, stirring frequently until softened: about 10 minutes. Add a pinch of salt while cooking to bring out their flavour.
5. Spread cream cheese on the crostinis and top with mushroom mixture. Add a touch of pepper to each if you like.

THESE CAN BE MADE THE MORNING OF THE PARTY AND KEPT COVERED IN THE FRIDGE. YOU WILL NEED TO HEAT THEM IN A PREHEATED OVEN AT 230°C FOR 1 MINUTE TO TAKE THE CHILL OFF.

HAVE A
Heart

MAKES 24

Your guests will swoon over these artichoke-heart crostinis. They are as smooth and sexy as Barry White.

1 long baguette

olive oil

1 x 400g can artichoke hearts, drained

4 tbsp pesto

a little grated Parmesan cheese

1. Preheat oven to 200°C. Cut baguette into ½ cm slices and arrange them on a baking sheet lined with parchment paper.
2. Brush the top of the crostinis with oil and bake for around 10 minutes until they are lightly toasted.
3. Purée the artichoke hearts and the pesto in a food processor until smooth. Spread on the crostinis. Garnish with a sprinkle of grated Parmesan.

THESE CAN BE MADE THE MORNING OF THE PARTY AND KEPT COVERED IN THE FRIDGE.

'When I read about the evils of drinking

I gave up reading.'

– Henny Youngman

PARIS

Stilton

These delicious crostinis will satisfy the poshest palates. They need to be served warm but are worth the effort as they are très elegant.

1 long baguette

olive oil

80g (2 tbsp) apricot jam

2 tbsp balsamic vinegar

24 dried figs, coarsely chopped

250g cream cheese, softened

110g Stilton

60g pecans, chopped

1. Preheat oven to 200°C. Cut baguette into ½ cm slices and arrange them on a baking sheet lined with parchment paper.
2. Brush the top of the crostinis with oil and bake for around 10 minutes until they are lightly toasted.
3. In a small saucepan, stir apricot jam and vinegar over low heat until blended. Add figs and cook over low heat for 5 minutes or until softened. Remove from heat.
4. Mix cream cheese and Stilton with a fork or in a blender.
5. Spread a generous layer of cheese mixture on the crostinis. Top with 1 heaped teaspoon fig mixture and ½ teaspoon chopped pecans.
6. Bake 3 to 5 minutes in the oven.
* An easier but still yummy option is simply to spread fig jam on a crostini. Put some blue cheese on top and serve cold.

YOU CAN PREPARE THESE THE MORNING OF THE PARTY AND BAKE JUST BEFORE YOUR GUESTS ARRIVE. SERVE WARM.

**SERVE WARM
MAKES 24**

Brie is the Kate Middleton of cheese. It's effortlessly elegant, just like these crostinis.

1 long baguette

olive oil

80g (2 tbsp) apricot jam

160g Brie

12 walnuts, halved

1. Preheat oven to 200°C. Cut baguette into ½ cm slices and arrange them on a baking sheet lined with parchment paper.
2. Brush the top of the crostinis with oil and bake for around 10 minutes until they are lightly toasted.
3. Spread the crostinis with apricot jam. Add a thin slice of Brie and put half a walnut on top. Put back in the oven for 3 minutes until the Brie is melted.
* You can substitute mango chutney for the apricot jam.

YOU CAN PREPARE THESE THE MORNING OF THE PARTY AND BAKE JUST BEFORE YOUR GUESTS ARRIVE. SERVE WARM.

Doughy Duvets

$\mathcal{A}$ nother super-easy yet scrumptious way to lay on the carbs is to wrap foodstuffs in little pastry comforters, which are the American take on Pigs in Blankets. You can wrap up anything in a puff-pastry duvet. I've included a bunch of easy recipes for hors d'oeuvres rolled in little sleeping bags or wrapped like tiny purses. But honestly, you could roll up mystery meat or almost anything in these pastry bundles and it would taste delicious. I keep a packet of puff-pastry in the freezer at all times in case I have unexpected guests or the Chippendales happen to stop by.

'You only live once, but if you do it right,

ONCE IS ENOUGH.'

– Mae West

PIGS IN
Pashminas

No cocktail party is complete without Pigs in Blankets or for the fashion cognoscenti Pigs in Pashminas, a classic dish that was all the rage at 1950s cocktail parties. They consist of cocktail sausages wrapped in puff pastry. You can also use frankfurters, mini smoked sausages or any other type. You can prepare the piggies up to a few hours in advance and bake at the last minute.

500g ready-rolled frozen puff pastry, thawed

24 cocktail sausages

2 eggs, beaten with 1 tsp water

1. Preheat oven to 190°C. Line a rimmed baking sheet with parchment paper.
2. Roll out two pastry sheets on to the parchment paper. Cut the sheets into 24 vertical strips, slightly smaller than the length of each sausage, about 2.5cm wide by 8cm long.
3. Place each sausage at the end of a pastry strip and roll it until the pastry overlaps about 1cm.
4. Arrange the pigs on the baking sheet seam side down. Use a pastry brush to paint each piggy with a little of the beaten egg yolk to give it a nice golden brown colour. Bake until golden brown: 12 to 15 minutes. Accompany with a mixture of equal parts mustard and honey, or ketchup.
* You can also wrap a small slice of cheese around the sausages or add a bit of grated Cheddar for even more flavour.

YOU CAN PREPARE THESE WELL IN ADVANCE AND FREEZE THEM IN A FREEZER BAG. DEFROST THEM OVERNIGHT IN THE FRIDGE, OR, IF YOU ARE IN A HURRY, YOU CAN PUT THEM IN THE OVEN FROZEN AND BAKE THEM A LITTLE LONGER: 15 TO 18 MINUTES.

CHICKS IN
Blankets

While less well known, Chicks in Blankets are just as delicious as any pashmina-wearing porkers. These tiny chicken sausages wrapped up in little doughy stoles are super-tasty.

500g ready-rolled frozen puff pastry, thawed

170g honey

120g Dijon mustard

24 mini chicken sausages

2 eggs, beaten with 1 tsp water

1. Preheat oven to 190°C. Line a rimmed baking sheet with parchment paper.
2. Roll out two pastry sheets on to the parchment paper. Cut the sheets into 24 vertical strips, slightly smaller than the length of each sausage, about 2.5cm wide by 8cm long.
3. Combine honey and Dijon in a small bowl. Spread honey mixture on each pastry strip. Save the rest of the honey mixture for serving.
4. Place each sausage at the end of a pastry strip and roll it until the pastry overlaps about 1cm.
5. Arrange the blankets on the baking sheet seam side down. Use a pastry brush to paint each chick with a little of the beaten egg yolk to give it a nice golden brown colour. Bake until golden brown: 12 to 15 minutes. Accompany with leftover honey and mustard mixture for dipping.

YOU CAN PREPARE THESE WELL IN ADVANCE AND FREEZE THEM IN A FREEZER BAG. DEFROST THEM OVERNIGHT IN THE FRIDGE, OR, IF YOU ARE IN A HURRY, YOU CAN PUT THEM IN THE OVEN FROZEN AND BAKE THEM A LITTLE LONGER: 15 TO 18 MINUTES.

SLEEPY
Prawns

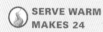

SERVE WARM
MAKES 24

These sensational sleepy prawns will have your guests salivating. They are a five-star hors d'oeuvre with a B&B price tag.

500g ready-rolled frozen puff pastry, thawed

250g cream cheese

1 tbsp curry powder

2 tbsp apricot jam

2 spring onions, chopped

24 large uncooked prawns, deveined and peeled (about 450g)

2 eggs, beaten with 1 tsp water

1. Preheat oven to 190°C. Line a rimmed baking sheet with parchment paper.
2. Roll out two pastry sheets on to the parchment paper. Cut the sheets into 24 vertical strips, about the length of the prawns less the tail and about 8cm long.
3. Combine cream cheese, curry powder, apricot jam and spring onions in a small bowl. Spread the cream cheese mixture on the pastry strip.
4. Place an uncooked prawn at the end of each pastry strip and roll it until the pastry overlaps about 1cm.
* Prawns should be cooked within 24 hours of buying them.
5. Arrange on the baking sheet seam side down. Use a pastry brush to paint each prawn with a little of the beaten egg yolk to give it a nice golden brown colour. Bake until golden brown: about 10 minutes.
* You can ditch the curry powder and apricot jam and use ½ tbsp East End Fish Seasoning mixed with the cream cheese.

YOU CAN PREPARE THESE THE MORNING OF THE PARTY AND REFRIGERATE COVERED. BAKE JUST BEFORE YOUR GUESTS ARRIVE.

SERVE WARM
MAKES 24

These little cheese purses are just darling. Your guests will eat them like they are going out of fashion.

500g ready-rolled frozen puff pastry, thawed

250g cream cheese, softened

2 spring onions, chopped finely

6 rashers streaky bacon, cooked and chopped

2 eggs, beaten with 1 tsp water

1. Preheat oven to 180°C. Line a rimmed baking sheet with parchment paper.
2. Roll out a pastry sheet on to a flat surface and cut into 12 squares, roughly 6cm each side. Repeat with the second sheet.
3. Combine cream cheese, spring onions and chopped cooked bacon.
4. Place a teaspoon of the cream cheese mixture in the centre of each pastry square.
5. Fold up all four corners of the pastry square and pinch together to form a small purse around the cheese.
6. Arrange on the baking sheet seam side up. Use a pastry brush to paint each purse with a little of the beaten egg yolk to give it a nice golden brown colour. Bake for 10 minutes or until the purses are golden brown.
* If you like, you can substitute 120g chopped ham for the bacon.

YOU CAN PREPARE THESE WELL IN ADVANCE AND FREEZE THEM IN A FREEZER BAG. YOU CAN DEFROST THEM OVERNIGHT IN THE FRIDGE, OR, IF YOU ARE IN A HURRY, YOU CAN PUT THEM IN THE OVEN FROZEN AND BAKE THEM A LITTLE LONGER: 15 TO 18 MINUTES.

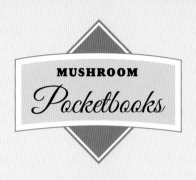

MUSHROOM
Pocketbooks

SERVE WARM
MAKES 24

Mushrooms have never been so chic. These fabulous fungi pocket books will provide a delicious accessory to your cocktail menu.

500g ready-rolled frozen puff pastry, thawed

225g mushrooms

2 tbsp butter or oil

250g cream cheese, softened

¼ tsp ground pepper

2 eggs, beaten with 1 tsp water

1. Preheat oven to 180°C. Line a rimmed baking sheet with parchment paper.
2. Roll out a pastry sheet on to a flat surface and cut into 12 squares, roughly 6cm each side. Repeat with the second sheet.
3. Wipe mushrooms clean, remove the stems and chop. Heat butter or oil in a frying pan over medium heat. Add the mushrooms and a pinch of salt and cook for about 10 minutes, stirring occasionally.
4. Blend cream cheese and mushrooms in a food processor. Sprinkle with pepper.
5. Place a teaspoon of the cream cheese mix in the centre of each pastry square.
6. Fold up all four corners of the pastry square to form a small purse around the cheese. Use a pastry brush to paint each pocketbook with a little of the beaten egg yolk to give it a nice golden brown colour.
7. Bake for 10 minutes or until the purses are golden brown.

YOU CAN PREPARE THESE WELL IN ADVANCE AND FREEZE THEM IN A FREEZER BAG. YOU CAN DEFROST THEM OVERNIGHT IN THE FRIDGE, OR, IF YOU ARE IN A HURRY, YOU CAN PUT THEM IN THE OVEN FROZEN AND BAKE THEM A LITTLE LONGER: 15 TO 18 MINUTES.

HOT JALAPEÑO
Handbags

These jalapeño handbags are hotter than Ibiza in August. If you don't like them too fiery then buy mild jalapeños.

> 500g ready-rolled frozen puff pastry, thawed
>
> 180g Cheddar cheese, grated
>
> 1 x 200g jar hot sliced jalapeño peppers
>
> 2 eggs, beaten with 1 tsp water

1. Preheat oven to 180°C. Line a rimmed baking sheet with parchment paper.
2. Roll out a pastry sheet on to a flat surface and cut into 12 squares, roughly 6cm square. Repeat with the second sheet.
3. Place a teaspoon of cheese in the centre of each pastry square and put two jalapeño slices in the middle.
4. Fold up all four corners of the pastry square to form a small purse around the cheese and jalapeño.
5. Arrange on a baking sheet. Use a pastry brush to paint each handbag with a little of the beaten egg yolk to give it a nice golden brown colour. Bake for 10 minutes until the hot handbags are a fashionable tan.

YOU CAN PREPARE THESE WELL IN ADVANCE AND FREEZE THEM IN A FREEZER BAG. YOU CAN DEFROST THEM OVERNIGHT IN THE FRIDGE, OR, IF YOU ARE IN A HURRY, YOU CAN PUT THEM IN THE OVEN FROZEN AND BAKE THEM A LITTLE LONGER: 15 TO 18 MINUTES.

BUFFALO CHICKEN
Backpack

These Buffalo Chicken Backpacks are bursting with flavour. They combine all my favourite food crushes in one naughty package. I suggest using a shop-bought rotisserie chicken to make it even easier.

500g ready-rolled frozen puff pastry, thawed

250g cream cheese, softened

½ whole roasted chicken, shredded

60ml (4 tbsp) Buffalo Wings sauce

60ml (4 tbsp) ranch dressing

120g Cheddar cheese, grated

2 eggs, beaten with 1 tsp water

1. Preheat oven to 180°C. Line a rimmed baking sheet with parchment paper.
2. Roll out a pastry sheet on to a flat surface and cut into 12 squares, roughly 6cm each side. Repeat with the second sheet.
3. In a bowl, stir shredded chicken, Buffalo sauce, ranch dressing and cheese till well blended.
4. Place a heaped teaspoon of the chicken mix in the middle of each pastry strip.
5. Fold up all four corners of the pastry square to form a small backpack. Arrange on a baking sheet. Use a pastry brush to paint each backpack with a little of the beaten egg yolk to give a nice golden brown colour.
6. Bake for 10 minutes or until the backpacks are golden brown.

YOU CAN PREPARE THESE WELL IN ADVANCE AND FREEZE THEM IN A FREEZER BAG. DEFROST THEM OVERNIGHT IN THE FRIDGE, OR, IF YOU ARE IN A HURRY, YOU CAN PUT THEM IN THE OVEN FROZEN AND BAKE THEM A LITTLE LONGER: 15 TO 18 MINUTES.

BEST SHYNESS CURE!

If you get a bit shy around new people, the best way to cure this is to imagine all your guests are reincarnated puppies! You won't be able to stop smiling or trying to cuddle them.

Meaty

Meat is the yang to alcohol's yin. It's important to have some meaty munchies – something substantial to line our stomachs and keep us on the vertical side of sober. I've also included seafood in here – the meat of the sea – for the non-carnivores.

'If God did not intend us to eat animals,

why did he make them out of meat?'

– John Cleese

MAMA'S
Meatballs

You can make these with minced chicken if you aren't a big beef fan.

olive oil

1 small onion, finely chopped

450g minced beef

1 tsp salt

¼ tsp ground pepper

1 egg

½ tsp Worcestershire sauce

60g Italian-seasoned breadcrumbs

2 tbsp grated Parmesan cheese

1. Preheat oven to 200°C. Line a rimmed baking sheet with parchment paper.
2. Heat a splash of oil in a frying pan over medium heat. Sauté onion until translucent.
3. Season beef with salt and pepper. In a large bowl, combine beef, egg, Worcestershire sauce, breadcrumbs, Parmesan and onion.
4. Shape the mixture into 24 small meatballs. Arrange 2.5cm apart on the baking sheet. Bake for 15 to 18 minutes until no longer pink in the centre.
5. Let cool for a few minutes and put each one on a toothpick. Accompany with some warm marinara or barbecue sauce.
* You can also serve these meatballs in mini-buns with a splash of barbecue sauce or ketchup. Flatten six burger buns with a rolling pin and cut each into four pieces. Place each meatball on a piece of bun, add a slice of cheese and top with another piece of bun.
*If you can't find Italian-seasoned breadcrumbs, simply mix 90g breadcrumbs with 1tbsp of Italian seasoning.

YOU CAN PREPARE THE MEATBALLS AND FREEZE UNCOOKED UP TO SIX MONTHS AHEAD. BAKE FROZEN AT 200°C FOR 20 MINUTES BEFORE SERVING. OR PREPARE A DAY OR TWO IN ADVANCE, REFRIGERATE COVERED AND BAKE BEFORE THE PARTY.

Lazy Ho
HOT MEATBALLS

The atomic combination of chilli sauce and cranberry sauce will send your tastebuds into orbit.

400g cranberry sauce

1 x 255g bottle Heinz Tomato Ketchup Chilli Sauce

1 x 400g packet frozen meatballs

1. Combine cranberry sauce and chilli sauce in a large saucepan over medium-low heat. Stir with a spoon until blended.
2. Bring to the boil and add frozen meatballs. Turn down heat and let simmer for 20 minutes.
3. Accompany with toothpicks.
* This recipe doesn't work as well with regular meatballs – the frozen ones are best.

COOK MEATBALLS JUST BEFORE YOUR GUESTS ARRIVE.

'My favourite animal is steak.'

– Fran Lebowitz

BAKED BUFFALO
Wings

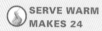
Buffalo chicken wings are so addictive they deserve their own 12-step programme. Make sure you put out a lot of napkins for guests to wipe their hands with as they are finger lickin' good.

24 chicken wings, tips removed

30g plain flour

½ tsp cayenne pepper

½ tsp salt

110g butter

120ml Buffalo Wings sauce

1. Cut each chicken wing at the joint to separate into two pieces.
2. Place the flour, cayenne and salt in a mixing bowl and blend. Coat wings with the spice mix, put on a plate and cover with cling film. Put in the fridge for at least 2 hours and up to 2 days.
3. Preheat the oven to 200°C. Line a rimmed baking sheet with parchment paper.
4. Melt the butter in a frying pan on low heat. In a small bowl, whisk together melted butter with Buffalo Wings sauce. Dip the wings into the sauce and butter mixture and put on the baking sheet in a single layer.
5. Bake for 15 minutes. Flip the wings and bake on the other side for another 15 minutes or until browned and tender. Accompany with ranch or blue cheese dressing.
* You can use some cooking spray on the parchment paper if you like as these wings are as sticky as Blu-Tack.

YOU CAN PREPARE THESE A DAY AHEAD AND COOK THEM JUST BEFORE YOUR GUESTS ARRIVE.

Wing It
ITALIAN STYLE

SERVE WARM
MAKES 24

The illicit union of Italian dressing and chicken wings is so mouthwatering it's like taking a bite out of Enrique Iglesias.

24 chicken wings, tips removed

250ml Italian dressing

1 tsp dried or fresh dill

1 tsp paprika

1. Cut each wing at the joint and separate into two pieces.
2. Combine Italian dressing, dill and paprika in a mixing bowl. Coat chicken wings with the dressing mix, put on a plate and cover with cling film. Put in the fridge for at least 2 hours and up to 2 days.
3. Preheat the oven to 200°C and line a rimmed baking sheet with parchment paper.
4. Bake for 15 minutes. Flip the wings and bake on the other side for another 15 or so minutes, until crispy on the outside and no longer pink in the centre.

YOU CAN PREPARE THESE A DAY AHEAD AND COOK THEM JUST BEFORE YOUR GUESTS ARRIVE.

BOURBON BEEF
Slider

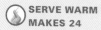 **SERVE WARM**
MAKES 24

The combination of beef, bourbon and BBQ sauce is like a ménage à trois in your mouth.

680g minced beef

1 tsp salt

1 tsp ground pepper

2 tbsp olive oil

1 large onion, diced

120ml bourbon

250ml barbecue sauce

½ jar (200g) jalapeño slices

6 burger buns

1. Season beef with salt and pepper and form into 24 small patties.
2. Heat oil in a medium frying pan over medium-high heat. Once the oil is hot, add the patties and cook until just about done in the middle: approximately 3 to 4 minutes each side. Remove the patties from the pan and set aside. Drain off all but 2 tablespoons of fat and return the pan to the stove.
3. Add diced onion to the frying pan and stir to cook: about 3 minutes. Take the pan off the heat before pouring in the bourbon (so it doesn't catch fire).
4. Return to the heat and stir, reducing the bourbon by half: about 2 to 3 minutes. Stir in the barbecue sauce and jalapeño slices.
5. Reduce heat to low and place the patties in the bourbon barbecue sauce to simmer, turning to coat, for a few minutes to absorb the flavour.
6. Flatten the burger buns with a rolling pin and cut each into four pieces. Place each patty on a piece of bun, spoon on some sauce and top with another piece of bun.

* You can use turkey or chicken if you don't want to use beef.

YOU WILL NEED TO COOK THESE JUST BEFORE THE PARTY. SERVE WARM.

BURGER JOINT
Slider

MAKES 24

These sliders are inspired by the ones from my local burger joint. Comfort food meets finger food in this mouthwatering mini-burger.

680g minced chuck steak

4 tbsp onion soup mix

1 egg

½ tsp ground pepper

pinch of salt

2 tbsp water

450g plain breadcrumbs

6 burger buns

24 sliced dill pickle rounds

1. Preheat oven to 200°C. Line a rimmed baking sheet with parchment paper.
2. Combine meat, soup mix, egg, pepper, salt, water and breadcrumbs in a large mixing bowl and mix well.
3. Shape the mixture into 24 small patties. Arrange about 2.5cm apart on the baking sheet. Bake for about 10 minutes until no longer pink in the centre.
4. Flatten the burger buns with a rolling pin and cut each one into four pieces. Place each patty on a piece of bun along with a pickle and top with another piece of bun.

YOU CAN PREPARE THESE PATTIES UP TO ONE DAY IN ADVANCE AND KEEP IN THE FRIDGE, COVERED. COOK JUST BEFORE THE PARTY.

Faux Gras

SERVES 24

Foie gras might be affordable for millionaires, but not for us regular folk. This 'faux' gras made from chicken livers is just as tasty but won't put your wallet in traction.

680g chicken livers

250ml milk

2 garlic cloves

2 tsp chopped fresh or 1 tsp dried thyme

½ tsp each salt and ground pepper

200g butter

1. Carefully trim the chicken livers, removing membranes and extra fat.
2. Place chicken livers, milk, garlic cloves, thyme, salt and pepper in a large bowl. Cover and refrigerate overnight.
3. Heat a frying pan to medium-hot. Remove the chicken livers from the milk mixture and shake off excess liquid, then pat dry. Cook the livers in the pan, until they are cooked through: about 4 minutes each side.
4. Place chicken livers in a food processor with the butter and purée until smooth.
5. Put the mixture into a serving bowl and leave in the fridge for 6 to 8 hours or until firm. Serve with baguette slices.

YOU CAN MAKE THE FAUX GRAS A DAY IN ADVANCE AND KEEP COVERED IN THE FRIDGE.

SERVE WARM
MAKES 24

These sausage meatballs are the Susan Boyle of the hors d'oeuvre world. This humble dish is surprisingly flavourful and will get your tastebuds singing.

450g pork sausagemeat

60g Italian-seasoned breadcrumbs

120g Cheddar cheese, grated

1 egg, lightly beaten

1. Heat oven to 190°C. Line a rimmed baking sheet with parchment paper.
2. Combine sausagemeat, breadcrumbs, cheese and egg in a large bowl. Mix until well blended.
3. Shape the mixture into 24 small balls. Arrange about 2.5cm apart on the baking sheet. Bake for 18 to 20 minutes or until golden brown, flipping them halfway through.
4. Let cool for a few minutes and put each one on a toothpick. Accompany with warm marinara sauce.
* If you can't find sausagemeat, you can get the butcher to take the meat out of sausage skins, or you can do this yourself with a pair of scissors.
* If you can't find Italian-seasoned breadcrumbs, simply mix 90g plain breadcrumbs with 1 tbsp Italian seasoning.

YOU CAN PREPARE THE SAUSAGE BALLS IN ADVANCE AND KEEP THEM IN THE FREEZER IN A FREEZER BAG. COOK THEM THE DAY BEFORE OR THE MORNING OF THE PARTY AND KEEP COVERED IN THE FRIDGE. REHEAT IN THE MICROWAVE BEFORE SERVING.

KICKASS
Kebabs

 **SERVE WARM**
MAKES 24

These kebabs are like sex on a stick, they are so scrumptious. They will have your guests salivating.

24 x 15cm wooden skewers

450g beef, lamb or chicken

3 cloves garlic, finely chopped

2 tsp paprika

1 tsp cumin

½ tsp turmeric

1 tsp salt

½ tsp ground pepper

80ml white wine

120ml olive oil

450g cherry tomatoes

1. Soak skewers in water for at least 20 minutes to prevent burning.
2. Cut the meat into small 2.5cm cubes. Combine the garlic, paprika, cumin, turmeric, salt, pepper, wine and oil in a bowl and mix well. Add the meat, cover and put in the fridge to marinate for at least 45 minutes but no longer than a few hours.
3. Thread meat on the skewers along with the cherry tomatoes.
4. Preheat the grill to high and place the rack 10–15cm below. Put the skewers on a baking sheet lined with aluminium foil and slide it under the grill.
5. Cook for 2 minutes, flip skewers, then cook the other side for another 2 minutes.
* You can also add a cube of feta to each skewer if you like.

YOU CAN PREPARE THESE THE MORNING OF THE PARTY BUT YOU WILL NEED TO REMEMBER TO TAKE THEM OUT OF THE MARINADE AFTER A FEW HOURS OR THEY WILL PARTIALLY COOK. GRILL THEM JUST BEFORE YOUR GUESTS ARRIVE.

Popcorn
CHICKEN

MAKES 24

These delicious chicken bites are like little firecrackers of flavour. It's like New Year's Eve for your mouth.

3 boneless chicken breasts

250ml buttermilk

2 tsp salt

125g plain flour

1½ tsp baking powder

2 tsp chilli powder

½ tsp dried oregano

½ tsp turmeric

1 tsp onion powder

½ tsp ground pepper

vegetable oil for frying

1. Cut the chicken breasts into equal bite-sized pieces. In a large bowl combine the chicken pieces, buttermilk and 1 teaspoon salt. Cover and chill in the fridge for at least 1 hour and up to 8 hours.
* After you've handled the chicken, make sure you wash your hands before you touch anything else. Salmonella is a bigger party killer than an Enya album.
2. In a separate bowl, combine flour, 1 teaspoon salt, baking powder, chilli powder, oregano, turmeric, onion powder and pepper.
3. Remove a few pieces of the chicken from the buttermilk marinade and shake off excess liquid. Place in the flour mixture and coat well.
4. Put oil in a medum-sized frying pan to a depth of about 1cm and heat over medium-high heat for about 1 minute. Be careful in case the oil splatters.
5. Place the chicken bites in the pan and cook for about 3 minutes per side or until golden brown and cooked through.
6. Place on kitchen paper to remove excess oil. Repeat with the remaining chicken.

PREPARE THE POPCORN CHICKEN THE MORNING OF THE PARTY AND COOK JUST BEFORE THE GUESTS ARRIVE. SERVE WITH BARBECUE SAUCE, HONEY MUSTARD OR KETCHUP.

POSH PRAWN *Mousse*

SERVES 24

This is the prawn version of foie gras. It's decadent and indulgent and will have your tastebuds doing somersaults.

300ml tomato soup

125g cream cheese

1 envelope unflavoured gelatin

60ml cold water

110g mayonnaise

4–5 spring onions, chopped

110g pre-cooked prawns

1. Heat the soup in a small saucepan over low heat. Cut up the cream cheese and fold into the soup. Stir with a whisk until blended.
2. Mix an envelope of gelatin with 60ml cold water and add to the soup mixture. Let cool slightly.
3. Fold in the mayonnaise, spring onions and prawns. Place the mixture in a bowl or ramekin (if small, you may need two) and chill, covered, in the fridge for several hours until firm.
4. Serve with Ritz crackers.

YOU CAN MAKE THIS THE DAY BEFORE THE PARTY AND KEEP IT IN THE FRIDGE. SERVE COLD WITH CRACKERS.

REMOVING RED WINE STAINS: The best way to remove red wine stains is by applying a mixture of equal parts hydrogen peroxide and soap or liquid detergent. The only thing this miracle mix won't remove is the stains on your reputation.

MINI CRAB *Cakes*

MAKES 24 SMALL CRAB CAKES

These miniature crab cakes will go down swimmingly at your next shindig.

225g canned crab meat,
   drained
110g mayonnaise
180g plain breadcrumbs
3 spring onions, thinly sliced
1 tsp East End Fish Seasoning
2 large eggs, lightly beaten
3 tbsp vegetable oil

Spicy Mayo Sauce
80g mayonnaise
1½ tbsp lemon juice
1 tbsp chilli sauce

1. In a medium bowl, mix all ingredients, apart from the oil, together.
2. Divide the mixture into 24 portions and use your hands to form small balls. Flatten the balls into small patties.
3. Heat a tablespoon of oil in a frying pan over medium-low heat and cook the crab cakes in batches for 3 to 4 minutes on each side or until golden brown.
4. Serve warm or at room temperature with a spicy mayo sauce made from mixing the mayonnaise, lemon juice and chilli sauce.
* You can serve these crab cakes in mini-buns accessorized with some iceberg lettuce and spicy mayo sauce or tartar sauce. Flatten six burger buns with a rolling pin and cut each into four pieces. Place each crab cake on a piece of bun, add sauce and a piece of lettuce and top with another bun.

YOU CAN PREPARE THE CRAB CAKES UP TO A DAY IN ADVANCE AND KEEP COVERED IN THE FRIDGE. COOK THE PATTIES THE MORNING OF THE PARTY AND REHEAT THEM IN THE MICROWAVE FOR ABOUT 30 SECONDS.

COCONUT
Prawns

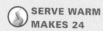

These tropical prawns will make you feel as if you are on holiday. Find a Man Friday to hand-feed them to you to add to the holiday vibe.

40g cornflour

1 tsp salt

¾ tsp cayenne pepper

160g flaked sweetened coconut

450g large prawns, peeled and deveined

3 egg whites, beaten until foamy

1. Preheat the oven to 190°C. Spray a baking sheet with cooking spray.
2. Mix cornflour, salt and cayenne pepper in a bowl. Pour coconut flakes into a separate bowl. Working with one prawn at a time, dredge it in the cornflour mixture, then dip it in the egg white, and roll it in the coconut, making sure to coat it well. Place on the prepared baking sheet, and repeat with the remaining prawns.
3. Bake prawns for 7–8 minutes per side, until golden brown.

YOU CAN PREPARE THE PRAWNS THE MORNING OF THE PARTY AND KEEP THEM IN THE FRIDGE COVERED. COOK THEM JUST BEFORE YOUR GUESTS ARRIVE. SERVE WITH SWEET CHILLI DIPPING SAUCE.

TIPSY TEQUILA
Prawns

Everything tastes better with a little tequila, including these soused prawns. Don't sneak too many tequila shots while you are making this tipsy dish, though, or your prawns may end up in need of rehab.

24 x 15cm wooden skewers

250ml tequila

120ml lime juice

1 tsp cayenne pepper

1 tsp chilli powder

1 tsp salt

2 tsp sugar

400g uncooked king prawns

olive oil, for sautéing

1. Combine tequila, lime juice, cayenne, chilli powder salt and sugar in a bowl and mix well. Add the prawns, cover and put in the fridge to marinate for at least 30 minutes but no longer than a few hours.
2. Drain the prawns from the marinade. Heat 1 tablespoon of oil in a medium frying pan and cook the prawns in batches, stirring or tossing frequently until pink and cooked through: 3 to 5 minutes.
3. Once cooled, thread on skewers and accompany with salsa.

THESE NEED TO BE MADE RIGHT BEFORE THE PARTY STARTS. IF THE PRAWNS ARE LEFT TOO LONG IN THE MARINADE, THE FRUIT ACID WILL PARTIALLY COOK THEM.

Bacony

*B*acon… is there anything it cannot do? It makes everything taste better, look better, feel better. It's the accessory *du jour* for any cocktail party. Better still, it's easy to get and even easier to cook. Bacon works fantastically with any number of foodstuffs – wrapped around them as little bacon stoles, stuffed inside or crumbled on top. Read on for some baconlicious ideas.

'Bacon is the answer.

'Who cares what the question is?'

– Anonymous-

Bring Home the Bacon

**EVERYTHING YOU EVER WANTED TO KNOW ABOUT COOKING
AND STORING BACON BUT WERE AFRAID TO ASK.**

COOKING BACON

If you are making a lot of bacon, I suggest baking it in the oven at 190°C for 15 to 25 minutes, depending on how crispy you like it. Make sure you put down foil or parchment paper on the baking sheet to absorb any mess.

You can also cook it in a frying pan over medium-high heat. Leave the bacon out for 5 minutes to take the chill off and put it in a cold pan. (If you put it in a hot pan you run the risk of scorching it.) The pan won't need oil as bacon is greasier than the Fonz's hairdo. Use tongs to flip the rashers when the bacon starts curling at the edges: about 3 to 5 minutes. Cook for a couple of minutes or so on the other side or until the right degree of doneness.

You can also cook your bacon in the microwave. I think this is the best method if you are only cooking a few rashers. Line a microwave-safe plate with a couple of sheets of kitchen paper and place the bacon on the plate in a single layer with no overlapping. Put another sheet of kitchen paper on top. Microwave on high for 2 to 3 minutes or until the desired degree of doneness. Bear in mind, the more bacon the longer the cooking time.

STORING BACON

I like to keep some bacon in the freezer at all times. The best way to store it in the freezer is wrapped in cling film and aluminium foil. Defrost it by putting it in the fridge overnight. If you are in a hurry, put it in the microwave in a microwave-safe dish. Click the defrost setting and put in the approximate weight of the bacon. Just make sure you take the bacon out before it starts to cook. Mmmmm… bacon.

DEVILS ON
Horseback

This classic hors d'oeuvre is devilishly delicious. Drunken Devils soak the prunes in red wine for a couple of hours before stuffing.

24 toothpicks

40g (1 tbsp) mango chutney or apricot jam

24 prunes, stoned

24 whole roasted almonds (about 25g)

12 thin slices streaky bacon, cut in half crosswise

1. Place toothpicks in a small bowl, cover with water and soak for 15 minutes to prevent them from burning.
2. Preheat oven to 190°C. Line a rimmed baking sheet with parchment paper.
3. Put a small dollop of chutney or apricot jam on each of the prunes and nestle an almond on top. Wrap each prune in a half-slice of bacon and secure with a toothpick.
4. Arrange on the baking sheet seam side down. Bake for 10 minutes. Take out of the oven, flip, and cook for another 8 to 10 minutes or until the bacon is cooked through.

YOU CAN ASSEMBLE THESE THE DAY BEFORE THE PARTY AND KEEP THEM IN THE FRIDGE, COVERED. BAKE THEM JUST BEFORE THE PARTY.

BACON
Bliss

These bacon-wrapped dates are so good that when you bite into them you will hear the music of the spheres.

24 toothpicks

24 dates, stoned

125g goat's cheese, softened

12 thin slices streaky bacon, cut in half crosswise

1. Place toothpicks in a small bowl, cover with water and soak for 15 minutes to prevent them from burning.
2. Preheat oven to 190°C. Line a rimmed baking sheet with parchment paper.
3. Cut each date lengthwise down the middle and fill the cavity with goat's cheese. Wrap each date in a half-slice of bacon and secure with a toothpick.
4. Arrange on the baking sheet seam side down. Bake for 10 minutes. Take out of the oven, flip, and cook for another 8 to 10 minutes or until the bacon is cooked through.
* You can use cream cheese in place of the goat's cheese if you like.

YOU CAN ASSEMBLE THESE THE DAY BEFORE THE PARTY AND KEEP THEM IN THE FRIDGE, COVERED. BAKE THEM JUST BEFORE THE PARTY.

APRICOT
Affair

The combination of dried apricots and bacon is so tempting, it could be the start of a new culinary affair.

24 toothpicks

85g (4 tbsp) maple syrup

12 thin slices streaky bacon, cut in half crosswise

24 dried apricots

1. Place toothpicks in a small bowl, cover with water and soak for 15 minutes to prevent them from burning.
2. Preheat oven to 190°C. Line a rimmed baking sheet with parchment paper.
3. Brush maple syrup on the inside of the bacon strips. Wrap each apricot in a half-slice of bacon and secure with a toothpick.
4. Arrange on the baking sheet seam side down. Bake for 10 minutes. Take out of the oven, flip, and cook for another 8 to 10 minutes or until the bacon is cooked through.

YOU CAN ASSEMBLE THESE THE DAY BEFORE THE PARTY AND KEEP THEM IN THE FRIDGE, COVERED. BAKE THEM JUST BEFORE THE PARTY.

BANANA-
Rama

SERVE WARM
MAKES 24

Soft banana swoons in the embrace of cripsy bacon. This delightful combination will titillate your tastebuds.

24 toothpicks

85g (4 tbsp) maple syrup

12 thin slices streaky bacon, cut in half crosswise

4 bananas

1. Place toothpicks in a small bowl, cover with water and soak for 15 minutes to prevent them from burning.
2. Preheat oven to190°C. Line a rimmed baking sheet with parchment paper.
3. Brush the maple syrup on the inside of the bacon strips. Cut each banana into six 2.5cm long slices. Wrap each banana piece in a half-slice of bacon and secure with a toothpick.
4. Arrange on the baking sheet seam side down. Bake for 10 minutes. Take out of the oven, flip, and cook for another 8 to 10 minutes or until the bacon is cooked through.

YOU CAN ASSEMBLE THESE THE DAY BEFORE THE PARTY AND KEEP THEM IN THE FRIDGE, COVERED. BAKE THEM JUST BEFORE THE PARTY.

I DON'T GIVE

a Fig

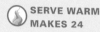

SERVE WARM
MAKES 24

You won't give a fig if anybody sees you scoffing seconds and even thirds of this hors d'oeuvre.

24 toothpicks

24 dried figs

12 thin slices streaky bacon, cut in half crosswise

24 almonds (optional)

1. Place toothpicks in a small bowl, cover with water and soak for 15 minutes to prevent them from burning.
2. Preheat oven to 190°C. Line a rimmed baking sheet with parchment paper.
3. Wrap each fig in a half-slice of bacon, adding an almond to the top of the fig before wrapping it if you want some extra crunch. Secure with a toothpick.
4. Arrange on the baking sheet seam side down. Bake for 10 minutes. Take out of the oven, flip, and cook for another 8 to 10 minutes or until the bacon is cooked through.

YOU CAN ASSEMBLE THESE THE DAY BEFORE THE PARTY AND KEEP THEM IN THE FRIDGE, COVERED. BAKE THEM JUST BEFORE THE PARTY.

Bawdy
BREADSTICKS

This is the easiest bacon hors d'oeuvre of all time and super-scrumptious.
Don't halve the bacon for this one. Use a whole thin strip.

24 thin slices streaky bacon

24 cheesy breadsticks

1. Preheat oven to 190°C. Line a rimmed baking sheet with parchment paper.
2. Wrap the bacon along the length of each cheesy breadstick until covered, leaving 1cm on the ends.
3. Arrange on the baking sheet seam side down. Bake for 8 minutes. Take out of the oven, flip, and cook for another 7 to 8 minutes or until the bacon is cooked through.

YOU CAN ASSEMBLE THESE THE DAY BEFORE THE PARTY AND KEEP THEM IN THE FRIDGE, COVERED. BAKE THEM JUST BEFORE THE PARTY.

TREASURE
Chestnuts

SERVE WARM
MAKES 24

The crunchy texture of water chestnuts goes perfectly with bacon. Mmmmm.

24 toothpicks

2 x 225g cans water chestnuts

12 thin slices streaky bacon, cut in half crosswise

1. Place toothpicks in a small bowl, cover with water and soak for 15 minutes to prevent them from burning.
2. Preheat oven to 190°C. Line a rimmed baking sheet with parchment paper.
3. Wrap each water chestnut in a half-slice of bacon and secure with a toothpick.
4. Arrange on the baking sheet seam side down. Bake for 10 minutes. Take out of the oven, flip, and cook for another 8 to 10 minutes or until the bacon is cooked through.

YOU CAN ASSEMBLE THESE THE DAY BEFORE THE PARTY AND KEEP THEM IN THE FRIDGE, COVERED. BAKE THEM JUST BEFORE THE PARTY.

BACON
Dogs

Bacon dogs are a perennial favourite in the pantheon of bacon-wrapped delights.

24 toothpicks

24 cocktail sausages

12 thin slices streaky bacon, cut in half crosswise

1. Place toothpicks in a small bowl, cover with water and soak for 15 minutes to prevent them from burning.
2. Preheat oven to 190°C. Line a rimmed baking sheet with parchment paper.
3. Wrap each sausage in a half-slice of bacon and secure with a toothpick.
4. Arrange on the baking sheet seam side down. Bake for 10 minutes. Take out of the oven, flip, and cook for another 8 to 10 minutes or until the bacon is cooked through.

YOU CAN ASSEMBLE THESE THE DAY BEFORE THE PARTY AND KEEP THEM IN THE FRIDGE, COVERED. BAKE THEM JUST BEFORE THE PARTY.

Jumping JALAPEÑOS

SERVE WARM
MAKES 24

These bacon-wrapped jalapeños will get your temperature rising. They are hotter than Alex Pettyfer.

24 toothpicks

12 fresh jalapeño peppers

250g cream cheese

12 thin slices streaky bacon, cut in half crosswise

1. Place toothpicks in a small bowl, cover with water and soak for 15 minutes to prevent them from burning.
2. Preheat oven to 190°C. Line a rimmed baking sheet with parchment paper.
3. Cut stems off peppers and cut them in half lengthwise. Remove seeds and ribs.
4. Fill each pepper half with cream cheese. Wrap each pepper half in a half-slice of bacon and secure with a toothpick.
5. Arrange on the baking sheet, seam side down. Bake for 10 minutes. Take out of the oven, flip, and cook for another 8 to 10 minutes or until the bacon is cooked through.

YOU CAN ASSEMBLE THESE THE DAY BEFORE THE PARTY AND KEEP THEM IN THE FRIDGE, COVERED. BAKE THEM JUST BEFORE THE PARTY.

Tempting
POTATO WEDGES

Potato wedges aren't just for kids. Wrapped in bacon, these precocious slivers of potato are food fit for lovers.

24 toothpicks

1 packet frozen potato wedges (750g)

12 thin slices streaky bacon, cut in half crosswise

1. Place toothpicks in a small bowl, cover with water and soak for 15 minutes to prevent them from burning.
2. Preheat oven to 190°C. Line a rimmed baking sheet with parchment paper.
3. Wrap each still-frozen potato wedge in a half-slice of bacon and secure with a toothpick.
4. Arrange on the baking sheet seam side down. Bake for 10 minutes, flip, and cook for another 8 to 10 minutes or until the bacon is cooked through.

YOU CAN ASSEMBLE THESE THE DAY BEFORE THE PARTY AND KEEP THEM IN THE FRIDGE, COVERED. BAKE THEM JUST BEFORE THE PARTY AND SERVE WARM.

Chocolate
BACON

MAKES 24

Bad boy bacon and sexy chocolate are so natural and naughty together they are like a burlesque show in your mouth. Your guests will be demanding an encore.

24 toothpicks

12 thin slices streaky bacon, cut in half crosswise

400g cooking chocolate

1. Place toothpicks in a small bowl, cover with water and soak for 15 minutes to prevent them from burning.
2. Preheat oven to 190°C. Line a rimmed baking sheet with parchment paper.
3. Roll the bacon into small logs, put a toothpick in each and arrange on the baking sheet.
4. Bake for 10 minutes, flip, then bake for another 10 minutes or until the bacon is cooked through. Put on a plate lined with kitchen paper and let cool.
5. Melt the chocolate in a small saucepan over the lowest possible heat, stirring frequently with a spoon until melted: about 3 to 4 minutes.
6. Remove the saucepan from the stove and dip the bacon in the chocolate to coat.
7. Arrange on a baking sheet and refrigerate for at least an hour to set the chocolate. Serve cold.
* You can also add sprinkles to the bacon logs after you have dipped them in the chocolate to add a bit of pizzazz.

STORE CHOCOLATE-DIPPED BACON IN AN AIRTIGHT CONTAINER IN THE REFRIGERATOR FOR UP TO THREE DAYS. SERVE COLD.

'Bacon is the meat candy of the world.'
– Katy Perry

'Friends are the bacon bits in the salad bowl of life.'
– Anonymous

'I used to have trouble choking down the pills I have to take for controlling my cholesterol, but it's a lot easier now that I wrap them in bacon.'
– Brad Simanek

'Do you want to eat my leftover bacon?'
– Said no one ever

'Do you want to know how good bacon is? To improve other food they wrap it in bacon.'
– Jim Gaffigan

'I had rather be shut up in a very modest cottage with my books, my family and a few old friends, dining on simple bacon, and letting the world roll on as it liked, than to occupy the most splendid post, which any human power can give.'
– Thomas Jefferson

'Either you like bacon or you are wrong.'
– Anonymous

'Life expectancy would grow by leaps and bounds if green vegetables tasted as good as bacon.'
– Doug Larson

'People who say nothing tastes as good as skinny feels have obviously never had bacon.'
– Anonymous

Classic

*Y*ou can't go past the classics. The Lazy Hostesses of yesteryear knew a thing or two about taking shortcuts in the kitchen as well as making time for nips of sherry. These finger-food staples have been around longer than Betty White and are still as delicious as ever. Like a black dress and pearls, some things never go out of style.

> '*I was on the low-carb diet for two weeks, and lost 2 inches from my smile.*'

SERVE WARM
MAKES 24

Delectable and adorable, these little mushrooms are a must on any party menu.

24 large (6cm-diameter) white mushrooms, stems removed

salt and ground pepper to taste

60g Italian-seasoned breadcrumbs

40g grated Parmesan cheese

2 garlic cloves, peeled and minced

2 tbsp chopped parsley or chives

3 tbsp olive oil

1. Preheat oven to 180°C. Line a rimmed baking sheet with parchment paper.
2. Wipe mushroom tops, clean and season the cavities (formed from removing the stems) with salt and pepper.
3. Combine the breadcrumbs, Parmesan, garlic, parsley (or chives) and olive oil in a small bowl and mix well.
4. Spoon the filling into the mushroom cavities and bake until heated through and golden on top: about 25 minutes.

*If you can't find Italian-seasoned breadcrumbs, simply mix 90g plain breadcrumbs with 1 tbsp Italian seasoning.

YOU CAN PREPARE THESE MUSHROOM MORSELS A MONTH OR SO AHEAD AND FREEZE THEM UNCOOKED. DEFROST THEM OVERNIGHT IN THE FRIDGE OR LEAVE THEM OUT TO DEFROST AT ROOM TEMPERATURE (ABOUT 20 MINUTES) BEFORE YOU COOK THEM.

SERVE WARM
MAKES 24

This carbtastic dish is the ultimate comfort food made chic. These are best made with baby red-skinned potatoes, but any baby potatoes will do.

12 baby potatoes, skins on

250g cream cheese

5 tbsp chopped chives or spring onions

8 rashers crisply cooked streaky bacon, finely chopped

salt and ground pepper to taste

1. Preheat oven to 180°C. Line a rimmed baking sheet with parchment paper.
2. Put the potatoes in a large saucepan filled with cold water. Let simmer (not boil) over medium heat for about 20 minutes, until a toothpick goes in easily.
3. Drain the potatoes and put on a plate to cool. Once they have reached room temperature, cut them in half and then cut a thin slice off the rounded base of each potato so it will sit flat.
4. Combine cream cheese, 4 tablespoons chives and bacon in a medium bowl. Add salt and pepper to taste.
5. Scoop out some of the centre of each potato with a small spoon or a melon-baller to make room for the stuffing. Fill each with 1 tablespoon or so of the cheese mixture.
6. Bake for 5 minutes. Garnish with the remaining chives.

YOU CAN PRE-PARBOIL THE POTATOES AND PRE-ASSEMBLE THE STUFFING BUT YOU WILL NEED TO STUFF AND COOK THESE ON THE DAY OF THE PARTY. YOU CAN DO THIS UP TO AN HOUR OR TWO BEFORE AND WARM THEM UP FOR 5 MINUTES IN A 200°C OVEN.

TRADITIONAL
Devilled
EGGS

MAKES 24 HALVES

There is a reason this classic dish has been around so long. It's so delicious it's devilish. Even better, it is usually served cold, which is great for lazy hostesses.

13 eggs (extra one for testing)
10 tbsp mayonnaise
3 tsp sweet relish

¼ red onion, sliced thin and fine
salt and pepper to taste
paprika to garnish

1. To hard-boil eggs, place them in a large saucepan, cover with cold water and bring to the boil. Simmer for 8 minutes.
2. Just prior to the 8-minute mark, scoop out your sacrificial test egg, pour cold water over it and check to see if it's cooked. Once you know the eggs are solid, immediately pour out the hot water and add cold water. This shocks the eggs and makes them easier to peel.
3. Peel the boiled eggs and discard the shells. Then slice them in half, lengthwise.
4. Remove the yolks and put in a mixing bowl. Add all the other ingredients and mix well. Fill the egg halves evenly with the mixture and garnish with paprika. Refrigerate and serve cold on a 'nest' of shredded lettuce.

THESE CAN BE MADE THE DAY BEFORE THE PARTY AND KEPT COVERED IN THE FRIDGE.

EASY

She-Devil

EGGS

This is a simplified version of the classic recipe. It has fewer ingredients but just as much flavour.

13 eggs (extra one for testing)

8 tbsp mayonnaise

2 tsp Dijon mustard

paprika to garnish

1. To hard-boil eggs, place them in a large saucepan, cover with cold water and bring to the boil. Simmer for 8 minutes.
2. Just prior to the 8-minute mark, scoop out your sacrificial test egg, pour cold water over it and check to see if it's cooked. Once you know the eggs are solid, immediately pour out the hot water and add cold water. This shocks the eggs and makes them easier to peel.
3. Peel the boiled eggs and discard the shells. Then slice them in half, lengthwise.
4. Remove the yolks and put in a mixing bowl. Add all the other ingredients and mix well. Fill the egg halves evenly with the mixture and garnish with paprika. Refrigerate and serve cold on a 'nest' of shredded lettuce.

THESE CAN BE MADE THE DAY BEFORE THE PARTY AND KEPT COVERED IN THE FRIDGE.

SAVOURY STUFFED
Celery

MAKES ABOUT 24

Who said celery was only for bunny rabbits and ribby models? When it's filled with cheese, it's positively wicked.

8 sticks celery

250g cream cheese, softened

pinch salt

pinch ground pepper

a few drops Worcestershire sauce

2 tbsp mayonnaise

pinch paprika (optional)

1. Wash celery sticks. Pat dry with kitchen paper and cut into 7.5cm lengths.
2. In a small bowl, use a fork to blend the cream cheese until smooth. Season with salt, pepper, paprika (if desired), a few drops of Worcestershire sauce and enough mayonnaise to make the mixture spreadable.
3. Fill the celery sticks with the cream mixture. If desired, sprinkle with paprika for extra colour. Arrange the stuffed celery on a platter and chill before serving.

THESE CAN BE MADE THE MORNING OF THE PARTY AND KEPT COVERED IN THE FRIDGE.

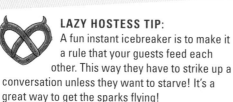

LAZY HOSTESS TIP:
A fun instant icebreaker is to make it a rule that your guests feed each other. This way they have to strike up a conversation unless they want to starve! It's a great way to get the sparks flying!

FLAMING MINI
Frittatas

My Gay Best Friend gave me this frittata recipe. Your friends will be eggstatic when they taste them.

2 tbsp olive oil	80g grated Parmesan cheese
1 medium onion, finely chopped	8 eggs
120g ham, chopped	salt and ½ tsp ground pepper

1. Preheat the oven to 180°C. Spray a 24-cup mini-muffin tin with cooking spray.
2. Heat oil in a frying pan over medium heat. Add chopped onion and sauté until translucent: about 3 minutes. In a bowl, combine onions, ham and cheese.
3. Break eggs into a medium bowl and season with salt and pepper. Whisk to blend.
4. Fill the mini-muffin cups evenly with the onion, ham and cheese mixture. Pour the egg mixture over each one to the top.
5. Bake for 12 to 15 minutes until cooked and the egg is set.
* If you like you can also add 250g button mushrooms, stemmed, chopped and sautéed.

IF YOU WANT TO GO THE EXTRA MILE, SERVE WITH A TINY DOLLOP OF SOUR CREAM ON TOP FOR EXTRA FLAVOUR AND A GARNISH OF CHOPPED CHIVES.

THESE CAN BE MADE THE MORNING OF THE PARTY AND KEPT COVERED IN THE FRIDGE. HEAT IN THE MICROWAVE BEFORE SERVING.

 **SERVE WARM**
MAKES 24

These pickles are inspired by a recipe from Hooters. They will be more popular than a lap dance at a stag party.

1 x 340g jar crinkle-cut gherkins

500ml buttermilk

250g plain flour

2 tsp salt

1 tsp paprika

2 tsp cajun spices

¼ tsp cayenne

vegetable oil

1. Drain the gherkins and place in a bowl with the buttermilk.
2. Combine all the dry ingredients in a separate bowl and mix well. Take the pickles out of the buttermilk, a handful at a time, and dredge with the seasoned flour.
3. Pour oil to a depth of 1cm in a medium frying pan and heat over medium-high heat for about 1 minute. Be careful in case the oil splatters.
4. Shake off excess flour and place the battered pickles in the hot oil. Be careful not to crowd them or they won't fry up crisp. Fry until golden brown: about 2 to 3 minutes.

YOU HAVE TO MAKE THESE JUST BEFORE SERVING AS OTHERWISE THEY WILL GO SOGGY. ACCOMPANY WITH RANCH DRESSING.

Cheat Sheet

If you get separation anxiety when you leave your couch, then you can always opt to order finger food delivered from your local supermarket. Even so, I recommend you make at least one or two simple hors d'oeuvres to give the menu a personal touch and help cure your cooking phobia. This way, you will begin to discover how easy and fun it really is. Not to mention it's far cheaper.

If you do want to order a few goodies, most supermarkets stock a variety of hors d'oeuvres, including cheese platters and oriental selections. Some examples of finger food they will likely have on hand are: cocktail sausages, mini meatballs, oriental, Indian or Mexican snacks, meat or vegetable samosas, vol au vents, mini-spring rolls, cheese straws, dips and crudités platters.

Make sure you discard all the empty packaging as evidence of your cheating. Simply transfer any shop-bought items on to your own platters to make them look like your own. You can also add your own laminated placemats with funny photos to the bottom of the platter to distract people from any lack of ornamentation. Add a sprig of parsley for garnish or a few flowers from the garden. Put sauces in little bowls so they look more elegant. And make up names for all your dishes, like 'Sexy Samosas' or 'Get Porked' or another moniker that makes them sound more alluring.

Host a Pot-luck Party

You can also host a pot-luck cocktail party and ask your guests to bring their signature cocktail dish along to add to the mix. Ask them to bring the recipe as well to add to your own repertoire. A pot-luck party will also give you a good idea of whom to recruit as your sous chef before your next soirée. Plus, bringing along their favourite recipe will give your guests something to talk about. Chances are they will also bundle up the leftovers to take home, meaning less cleaning-up for you.

You could even give out a prize for the best hors d'oeuvre. Everyone loves a little recognition. I've seen friends channel Gwyneth Paltrow at the Oscars as they tearfully gush their thanks for winning a frozen chook in a raffle. Winning anything, however crappy, is a secret thrill. Let everyone vote on the best dish and then toast the winner.

As far as prizes, the possibilities are limitless. It could be a kiss from the host, a pitcher of your signature cocktail, an oversized cocktail glass or a guaranteed invite to your next shindig (and a role as sous chef). Just make sure you get your hands on that recipe. And then send it to me.

If you are game, you could do the same with cocktails and taste-test your friends' favourite tipples to see which one wins the battle of the bevvies. Be prepared, though: this is a pretty quick way to get plastered. Try to serve each cocktail sample on a smaller scale than you usually would for tasting or you might end up seeing stars.

Pot-luck cocktails can be exciting if everybody really tries to whet each other's palates with their favourite drink ever. You might just find the sip of your life this way – that one glorious alchemical potion that, from the very first quaff, transforms your life from grey to technicolour. It will also give guests something to talk about as they rhapsodize about their elixir. You can also encourage guests to talk about their best and most embarrassing bar stories. All great stories begin with a cocktail.

'Give a prize for the best hors d'oeuvre.
EVERYONE loves a little recognition.' ♥

Cocktail Party 999

Surprise guests can strike fear in the heart of even the most steely hostess. Fear not. Here is your emergency cocktail-party plan. Just add vodka!

So the great unwashed, the motley crew you call your friends, have turned up at the door for a surprise visit like a swarm of locusts looking for food and sustenance. What do you do? Bolt the door, staple yourself to the lounge and hook yourself up to an intravenous Chardonnay? Curl up in the foetal position and hide under your feathered duvet? No, no, no! There is no longer any need for anxiety if you are called on to host an impromptu party. You are now a card-carrying cocktail-party queen and can entertain even unexpected guests with ease.

'We know you are there.
We can hear you drinking.'

Once you have done your HOmework and conquered your kitchen, you will be prepared to throw an instant cocktail party – just add vodka! It will be no problem if a bunch of nocturnal nomads arrives unannounced. Put out some snacks while you don a party frock, heels and a sexy apron. Grab at least one of your guests to help you assemble some delicacies. No Lazy Hostess ever spends time in the kitchen solo. It's a place to socialize not sweat it out. More hands mean less time. Put someone in charge of music and throw together some quick hors d'oeuvres.

Rainy-day Party Prep

For the same reason that you should always wear nice underwear (because you just never know), it's a good idea to be prepared for fate to come knocking at your door. In this vein, it's time you befriended your freezer. Stockpile it in readiness for a social onslaught. Prior to destiny landing on your doorstep, spend a rainy day in the kitchen making freezable finger foods. This way you will always have a few delectable hors d'oeuvres already on hand. Defrost and hey presto! You are ready to rumba.

Wait for a drizzly day and ask a friend over to assist you in assembling these dishes. Put on my 'Get Cooking' playlist, bust open the vino and don your apron. You can prepare Party Puffs, Pigs in Pashminas or Chicks in Blankets, Cheese Purses or Stuffed Mushrooms in advance, defrost and cook them according to the recipes in this section. You can also prepare Mama's Meatballs or the scrumptious Stargazing Sausage Balls in advance and freeze these in a freezer bag, then defrost according to our scrupulous directions. You can buy frozen meatballs and pop them in the freezer in readiness for making Lazy Ho Hot Meatballs at a moment's notice. If you spend a rainy day preparing for fun, you could literally defrost and heat your way to an instant cocktail party.

Apart from frozen victuals, here is a suggested instant menu you can put together from a scant list of staples and a quick trip to the corner shop without putting too much of a dent in your purse. No need to let your forever famished friends eat you out of house and home. If you never buy anything else, you will be able to make do with these standbys even if you had to host a cocktail party in a nuclear bunker.

For snacks, stick to potato crisps and sour cream onion dip (page 131). Next whip up the Potato-crisp Crusted Cheese Balls and put them in the freezer for 10 minutes to firm up (page 141). Quickly toast some baguette rounds to put together the Easy-peasy Crostini (page 152), pop the Pigs in Pashminas (page 162) in the oven, along with the Bawdy Breadsticks (page 195). And lastly hard-boil the eggs for Easy She-Devil Eggs (page 207).

Even if you make your whole cocktail party from scratch, this should take you less than an hour if you don't stop to swig too much Chardonnay. The basic shopping list for these quick and easy finger foods is given overleaf.

EMERGENCY
Supplies

CHANCES ARE MOST OF THESE SUPPLIES WILL ALREADY BE LYING AROUND IN YOUR KITCHEN AND YOU WILL JUST HAVE TO SUPPLEMENT WITH A FEW ITEMS FROM THE CORNER SHOP.

Pantry
Baguette
Olive oil
Potato crisps
Plain flour
Packet instant onion soup
Crackers
Honey
Ketchup
Cheesy breadsticks
Sun-dried tomatoes
Chilli sauce
Salt
Ground pepper
Nutmeg
Paprika

Freezer
Cocktail sausages
Bacon

Fridge
Milk
120g butter
Tub sour cream
Tub cream cheese
Cheddar cheese
Frozen puff pastry
Sun-dried tomatoes
1 dozen eggs
Mayonnaise
Dijon mustard
Cranberry sauce

Just Add Vodka!

I suggest making sure you have a couple of emergency bottles of wine on hand at all times. I buy my Chardonnay by the intravenous drip if not the caseload, but then I'm a total wino and administer this medicinal beverage on a nightly basis lest reality set in. Six o'clock in my abode is known as 'wine o'clock'. And sometimes if it's been a really long day, I ring one of my international friends so I can toast them in their time zone. A little vino is like a rainbow in a glass. It brightens the drabbest day.

It's also essential to have some vodka in the freezer as it's the most versatile of spirits. It's the alcoholic version of the Beatles – everyone loves it. Apart from wine and vodka, keep some ice water in the fridge to dilute your mixes. And have some ice on hand for those who like their drinks on the rocks. Some tonic water is also good to keep on standby, as it's a good alternative for those who don't like mixes. But don't panic if you emptied your drinks cupboard on your last bender: just pass around the hat and send a friend out on an emergency booze run.

I suggest sticking to two-ingredient signature cocktails for instant cocktail parties. It's all about the art of simplicity. Stick to vodka and one other ingredient. You could opt for a vodka martini (page 121) or a vodka gimlet (page 109). Or mint your own drink according to what you have on hand or within easy access.

You can mix vodka with almost any soft drink, juice or ginger ale in a ratio of about 1:3 to create a yummy potion. Mix up your own concoction for a pitcher drink and leave out whatever mixers you have on hand along with the vodka so your friends can also make their own vodka cocktail. Then all that's left to do is crank up the soundtrack and party.

'Once we hit 40, women only have about four taste buds left: one for vodka, one for wine, one for cheese, and one for chocolate.'

– Gina Barreca

'I believe that if life gives you lemons, you should make lemonade... And try to find somebody whose life has given them vodka, and have a party.'

– Ron White

'A good man can make you feel sexy, strong and able to take on the world... Oh sorry that's vodka... vodka does that.'

– Anonymous

'I have a punishing workout regimen. Every day I do one to three minutes on a treadmill, then I lie down, drink a glass of vodka and smoke a cigarette.'

– Anthony Hopkins

'No Long Islands or margaritas when you drink. It has to be straight vodka.'

– Nicole Polizzi

'That wasn't me texting at 3am. That was vodka.'

– All my girlfriends one night or other

'There are only two absolutes in life: friends and vodka. And the best times usually involve both.'

– Unknown

All good things must come to an end, even sizzling soirées.

Read on for some helpful tips on getting guests
to go bye-byes, luring a likely Romeo to your lair
and surviving the morning after.

The After Party

Getting Guests to Go Home

I don't know about your social circle, but give my friends a cocktail or two and most of them would move in for a week. It's easier to remove a bunion then get some of my buddies to go bye-byes. Ever the gracious hostess, I don't like to resort to threats or brute force, so I've had to develop a few strategies to get the rabble to hit the road.

1. THE FIRST TRICK is to stop serving drinks and offer guests coffee. I put my alcohol well out of sight as some of my cocktail-swilling comrades can sniff out liquor better than a basset hound. I always serve decaf but tell them it's caffeinated. A caterer taught me this trick. The real stuff will wake them up and give them a second wind and next thing you know the party will re-ignite.

2. TURN THE LIGHTS UP. Your guests will be about as happy as a bunch of vampires on a paper run. Then start gathering glasses and dishes and emptying the bins. Ask the remaining guests to help you sort out the post-party debris, and this should have most of them planning their imminent departure.

3. THE LAST RESORT and never-fail strategy is my party-killing 'Sayonara Sweeties' playlist. Make sure you put on a set of earmuffs or you may end up joining the mass exodus. These

TEN WAYS TO SAY TA-TA

Ciao

Arrivederci

Hasta la vista

Auf Wiedersehen

Au revoir

Adiõs

Sayonara

Toodles

Hit the road Jack (or Jill)

Out! Scram! Shoo!

mood-killing tunes include 'Time to Say Goodbye', 'Kumbaya My Lord', the entire soundtrack of *Godspell*, the lullaby from *Rosemary's Baby* and a selection of organ music. Go to babescott. com for these infallible goodbye grooves.

Boudoir Chic

Hopefully, you will have found some likely hunk to fall under the host, and in this event, you'll want to be prepared. Slipping into an oversized T-shirt and granny pants will puncture the mood quicker than a cold spoon. Firstly, make sure when you are sprucing up your abode you pay some attention to the boudoir. Make sure you have clean fresh sheets, and it's relatively tidy.

You don't want your bedroom to look like Bon Jovi has been staying there for a week (even if the band just left).

I also recommend ambient lighting. I'd use lamps rather than ceiling lights. You want that soft movie-star glow with just enough wattage to get around without the aid of a guide dog. I try to make my bedroom as dark as possible, like a *film noir* with me playing a low-rent Rita Hayworth. On that note, make sure you have blinds or curtains to stop the sun streaming in. Bright morning light has the same effect on romance as it does on Dracula.

♥ **BEDROOM ETIQUETTE:** *It's extremely rude to answer the phone during coitus.* **DON'T PICK UP**, *unless it's Adam Levine.*

Marilyn Monroe may have got away with only Chanel No. 5 on in bed, but for us mere mortals seductive lingerie is far more becoming than being completely in the buff. It's also nice to leave a little to the imagination, similar to how the beautiful packaging on a box of truffles enhances the appetite. Make sure you have a sexy négligée and nice panties to wear for your after-hours amour. A matching push-up bra that defies gravity is also advisable. As the truism goes: 'It's better for your cup to be half full than half empty.'

If you're game, you can even consider stockings and garters. They never fail to excite the imagination. I have a selection of get-lucky lingerie and a black silky bathrobe for just such occasions. It's a nice touch if you have a hotel-style bathrobe handy for your Midnight Romeo. A smoking jacket is even sexier.

Trying to climb out of Spanx is as sexy as unravelling miles of surgical tape, so I make sure to have my after-hours outfit at the ready so I can slip into it quickly before my amour discovers I'm bandaged tighter than Tutankhamen. And don't forget contraception. You don't want a few too many martinis to end up in a trip to the maternity ward.

And think about what you encase your feet in. They can be overlooked when it comes to the erogenous zones. This is why a pre-party pedicure is mandatory. Dinosaur toes are an instant libido-killer. There's nothing sexier in my opinion than wearing stilettos in the bedroom. These man-slaying shoes were designed to simulate the shape of a woman's feet during climax, and there is nothing more flattering to the tootsies. They also elongate the legs and perform instant liposuction on your thighs. If you don't want to wear high shoes, or if your date is shorter than Warwick Davis, kitten-heeled slippers are also sexy to strut about in. Whatever you do, don't slip into a pair of Ugg boots when you traipse about – or I'm going to come over and shake you. There's

'I'm the girl who lost her reputation and never missed it.'

– Mae West

no point going to the effort of looking like a supernova all night only to climb into bed looking like a bag lady.

Apart from naughty nightwear, a sexy soundtrack is key to getting you in the mood for love. I've put together a 'Midnight Romeo' playlist that'll definitely get the temperature rising (among other things).

As for nightcaps, my favourite potion for seduction is strawberry-infused vodka. I call this Va-Va Voom Vodka for its aphrodisiac effect. It's like Viagra in a glass. Simply put 250g of freshly washed, stemmed strawberries along with 620ml of vodka in a large glass jar and let this sit for 2 to 5 days. Strain and store in the fridge or freezer in a sealed container. Cocktails are best served ice-cold, so put a couple of tumblers in the fridge to chill earlier in the night or put the glasses in the freezer for 15 minutes up to a couple of hours. A last-minute strategy to chill the glasses is to fill them with ice, swirl and then empty the ice before you pour your drinks.

When you are ready to serve, put a few ice cubes in your chilled tumblers and pour over 60ml of the strawberry-infused vodka. Garnish with a strawberry if you have any on hand. This alluring elixir can also be reinvented as a delicious daytime drink for your girlfriends, simply by adding ginger ale in a ratio of 1 part strawberry vodka to 3 parts ginger ale. Simply combine strawberry vodka and ginger ale in a tumbler and add 3 or 4 cubes of ice.

If your squeeze has a sweet tooth, another super-sexy cocktail is bubbly served with a teaspoon of strawberry sorbet. Simply put the sorbet in the bottom of a champagne flute and then pour Brut sparkling wine on top. There's no need to stir or to pre-chill the glasses. Just keep your sparkling wine in an ice bucket when you take it out of the fridge to keep it cold. This sensuous sip is guaranteed to hit his sweet spots.

Your sugar daddy will totally swoon if you complement this lustful libation with some strawberries dipped in chocolate. Simply melt some cooking chocolate in a small saucepan over the lowest possible heat, stirring frequently with a spoon until melted: about 3 to 4 minutes. Dip the strawberries in the chocolate and put them in the freezer on a plate lined with parchment paper to firm up for 15 minutes. He will be eating out of your hand.

Another great option for midnight munchies is assembling a quick cheese plate with whatever cheeses you have left over. You can accessorize the plate with dried fruit, strawberries or grapes. You may even get your amour to hand-feed you the latter. A small bowl of honey or fig jam is also a nice touch to complement the cheese. Serve with some leftover crackers or baguette slices.

♥ **BEDROOM ETIQUETTE:** *Don't call out someone else's name during the throes of passion. It's very off-putting. If you've forgotten his moniker, just call him* **'STUDMUFFIN.'**

Make sure you also smell as fragrant as a rose before retiring to the boudoir. Chances are it's been a long hot night on the dance floor so take a quick shower and apply a subtle perfume. Perhaps you and your flirtatious friend will even share a shower. It's a great way to conserve water. Baths are also delicious. Have some bubble bath and tea lights handy in case you and Romeo relax in the tub together. Clean your pearly whites and have some mints handy by the bed in case your morning breath is reminiscent of the Scottish & Newcastle Brewery.

Have a spare toothbrush and towel on hand for your man *du jour*. And whatever you do, make sure there's plenty of toilet paper. I'd also leave a small stash of make-up there for the morning – eyeliner, mascara, tinted moisturizer and lip gloss – just the minimum you need to give Mother Nature a helping hand. Lastly, make sure you turn your mobile phone to vibrate in case one of your crazy cocktail-fuelled friends drunk-dials. The only sound you should be able to hear is Casanova's heavy breathing. Now you've set the scene for seduction, you and your consort should be ready to rewrite the Kama Sutra.

If your date stays for breakfast, spiked coffee is a sexy way to start the day. Forget decaf and use fresh percolated coffee if you can. It's worth the effort. I'm not even human till I've had my morning caffeine fix. Depending on what you have on hand and what you and your overnight guest prefer, some ideal spirits to give your coffee a kick are Kahlua, Grand Marnier, Amaretto or even bourbon. Simply add 30ml to each cup of your morning brew. Baileys Irish coffee also makes a seductive breakfast beverage. Just add 30ml of Baileys to your coffee and top with whipped cream. I always have whipped cream in the fridge – it doubles as a dessert and a bedroom accessory.

The best way to keep a man in your lair is to water *and feed* him. And by now you will both be in dire need of some hangover-curing fare. The antidote you both need is *bacon*. This miracle meat will not only grease your stomach but is sex in a skillet. Preheat the oven to 190°C and lay eight or so rashers of bacon on a rimmed baking sheet lined with parchment paper. Bake until the bacon is beginning to brown: around 15 minutes. Take the bacon out of the oven and brush the top of each rasher with maple syrup, then bake for another 3 to 5 minutes. Perhaps scramble some eggs to go with it. When he tastes that bacon along with his spiked coffee I'd be surprised if he doesn't propose to you. The stuff is culinary voodoo.

French toast is also great morning flirt fare. It's also best made with slightly stale bread, so you can use leftover baguette slices. To make this titillating toast, beat together 1 egg, 180ml milk, 1 teaspoon cinnamon, 1 teaspoon vanilla extract and a pinch of salt in a bowl. Heat a lightly oiled frying pan over medium heat. Soak the baguette slices in the egg mixture for 20 seconds on each side, or until thoroughly coated. Cook the baguette rounds on both sides until lightly browned and crisp, and serve warm.

Before he leaves, spray your party card with a light dose of your perfume and give it to him. If you can, try to get a quick snap of him to add to your album of the evening and to perhaps show off to your after-party posse. After all, you have a reputation to live down to.

MY FAVOURITE COME-ON LINE: 'You'll do.'

**HAVE YOUR SIREN SURVIVAL KIT
AT THE READY.**

Food for Love

Va-Va Voom Vodka

Bubbly

Strawberry sorbet

Strawberries dipped in chocolate

Whipped cream

Coffee, spiked with Baileys or
    your preferred poison

Bacon

Maple syrup

Eggs

Milk, full cream

Leftover baguette

Sugar

Cinnamon

Vanilla

Femme Fatale Fashion

Sexy négligée

Lacy panties

Cleavage-enhancing bra

Sexy shoes or
    kitten-heeled slippers

Seductive bathrobe

Tea lights and bubble bath
    for bathroom

Spare toothbrush

Mints for the bedside

Contraception

'It's not the men in your life that matters:

it's the life in your men.'

– Mae West

Cocktail-fuelled Cleaning Party

There's nothing quite as sobering as waking up to a trashed apartment on your own. It's an experience that should be shared – like a moon landing or Armageddon. The shock of emerging from a martini-induced coma to a total mess can cause irreversible psychological damage. However, waking up with company transforms the whole experience into a hilarious trip down memory lane and a communal clean-up rather than a hangover-frazzled chore.

Ideally, you will have lured some likely Casanova into your lair to enjoy the rest of the evening and help you work off all those cocktails with some HOrizontal folk dancing. But just in case Romeo didn't show up, have a friend on standby who is happy to stay over. And if you are privileging some likely stud with your party favours – then suggest your friend show up late morning instead to help clear the debris and to conduct a party post-mortem.

Pick a friend who is not only a whole lot of fun but *helpful*. Someone who doesn't mind rolling up their sleeves and knows the end of a broom from their big toe. If you have to, tell them you're going to post every one of their most unflattering party photos on Facebook with creative captions unless they lend a hand. And tag them for good measure. (Evil, I know – but effective.)

You probably won't have to resort to this. A cocktail-fuelled cleaning party can be just as enjoyable as the night before, if not more so. It's like an aerobic workout with kitchen gloves. If you feel inclined, you can even ask a few more friends to join the Febreze-wielding fray. I would ask the same posse you persuaded to help you briefly tidy before you retired to the boudoir the evening before. While I don't advocate doing all the cleaning at the tail end of the party, you definitely want to do a little clearing and rescue any leftover foodstuffs as well as every little drop of precious alcohol.

The best way to get your friends' clean freak on is to pump up the 'Dance (aka Clean) Your Ass Off' party playlist and to feed and water them. My friends will do almost anything for a free cocktail and a cook-up. It's the same principle Pavlov employed – they hear that cocktail shaker and they start salivating. Let them happily pick up bottles, glasses and get things gleaming while you and your kitchen co-pilot get to the stovetop to create some hair-of-the-dog cocktails and morning-after fare.

I wouldn't advise serving wine. It makes everyone want to sit around and wax sentimental, whereas bubbly or vodka gets people moving (read vacuuming). Vodka is my preferred post-party potion – they could use this feisty spirit to fuel the space shuttle, it injects so much energy into any vehicle it enters. It will get your posse cleaning like they were possessed. Of course, a Bloody Mary works well (although I like to call it the Bloody Merry).

Feel free to mint your own Bloody Brenda or whatever your

own version is of this hair-of-the-dog highball. Mix vodka and tomato juice and add whatever else you like to spice it up, whether a pinch of cayenne pepper or an epithet or two. Another easy after-party mix is the basic no-frills mimosa, a brunch staple. Half orange juice, half Brut sparkling wine, it's a drink just like us divas – part human, part divine. Remind yourself of this as you sip and stop feeling sub-human. You can add ice if you so desire and then let out a sigh as your siren super-powers return.

Bloody Merry

45ml vodka	2 dashes Worcestershire sauce
120ml tomato juice	4 dashes Tabasco
1½ tsp lemon juice	pinch of salt and pepper

Combine all ingredients in a mixing glass, then strain into an ice-filled pint glass or a red-wine glass. Garnish with a lemon wedge or a high-pitched giggle. If you are a big tequila tippler, you can create a Bloody Maria instead. This has 30ml tequila, 60ml of tomato juice and a dash of lemon juice, Tabasco and celery salt. Then simply combine as per the Bloody Merry.

Once the place starts looking less like a construction site and more like a queenly casa, then serve up a buffet of leftovers to your clean-up crew. Heat up everything you can find in your fridge, whether bacon-wrapped dates, Pigs in Blankets or Mama's

Meatballs. If there is any leftover dip, bring that out too or quickly mix another one with a packet soup mix and sour cream. Perhaps buy a fresh baguette at the local shop to slice up and serve with your victuals.

After your repast and a few refills, you and your inner circle can recount the events of the night before and embellish them. As Marilyn Monroe once said: 'It's all make believe anyway.' This is the perfect time to revisit your Cocktail Party Guest Book, full of compliments to the hostess, odes to the evening and inspired mantras to the martini gods. I use this book as a scrapbook of memories of the night (albeit rosé-tinted ones). Flip through your party snaps and select the most humorous ones to add to this album of debauchery and have your friends help you mint some cheeky captions.

It's all about capturing those priceless party moments and recording your queenliness for posterity (not to mention collecting material for those hefty ransom notes). As Oscar Wilde said: 'I never travel without my diary. One should always have something sensational to read in the train.' Your party memoir should be just as scintillating.

'You'll always be my friend, you know too much.'

– Anonymous

Acknowledgements

I'd like to thank my agent, the folks at Central Casting, the Academy... Oh wait, wrong speech. . . I don't have an agent, and, to paraphrase Groucho Marx, 'I wouldn't want to be a member of any academy that would accept me.' But seriously, there are some people I have to thank profusely, without whom this book would not have been possible.

Writing a book is a lot like throwing a soirée. They both involve copious amounts of cocktails, plentiful snacks, loud music and the counselling of close friends. (I may not be an actress but I am a drama queen.) It also involves a lot of delegating. I can't draw or design, and I don't like being in the kitchen all by myself. I'm convinced it's meant to be a communal place where you can conspire with your Chardonnay Support Group, taste, test, tipple and tell tales.

Firstly, I'd like to thank the wonderful team at Transworld Publishers for their belief in the book and their tireless support in bringing it to fruition. A big sloppy kiss goes to Chrissy Charalambides for discovering the Lazy Hostess on Twitter. (Yes, it all started with a tweet.) I'm also indebted to my fabulous editor Michelle Signore who really got the book from the get-go and who has been the best creative collaborator a writer could hope for. I'd also like to shout-out to the world's best book publicist Elizabeth Masters for her unstinting efforts to pimp this PR-ho.

As far as banging the drum, PR Diva Sophie Cross was also instrumental in getting the word out. A big air-kiss goes to Jennifer Pullinger for her savvy advice. The next big hug goes to Christa Bourg, my literary mentor and the calm in my perpetual storm. She helped me develop the book from a glint in my eye to a luminous tome and was such an endless source of wit and wisdom.

I'd also like to thank sexy chef Dave Hart and fellow kitchen vixen Rebecca Elman for helping me test-drive all the recipes and tickling my funny bone. And I'd like to raise a tipple to Charles Pierce for his culinary suggestions as well as mixologist Brendan Cullen who helped me taste test some of the Signature Sips.

I absolutely have to give a shout-out to my extremely talented designers, Stephanie and John Stislow and Graeme Andrew. They really know how to put on the ritz when it comes to the printed page. Thanks to their style savvy, *The Lazy Hostess* is one of the best-dressed tomes to hit town. I'd also like to thank Tina Sbrigato who designed my website and all my branding bric-a-brac.

A huge bear hug goes to Michael Thibeault at ArtRep for his unwavering support and for providing the illustrative talent I needed to bring this book to life. On that note, I want to give a big squeeze to the amazingly gifted Chuck Gonzales for his divine illustrations. If Michelangelo and Matt Groening had a love child, it would be Chuck. His bootylicious images are the ultimate in 2 Double D. I'd like to toast the incredible talent of ArtRep's Benjy Brooke and Mike Burakoff who created my HOlarious trailer, which can only be described as Quentin Tarantino meets Jessica Rabbit. You guys rock!

A big thanks to everyone else who has been involved in *The Lazy Hostess*, including Gracey Newman, Rae Votta, Kelly Gabrysch, Steve Wanczyk, Madeline Merrill and all of the cocktail-swilling cognoscenti who helped transform this book from a tipsy idea into a reality. As we say in my native Australia:

'I love youse all.' ❤

Index